Happy Cooking ♡

Culinary greetings from

HOLLAND AMERICA LINE

HOLLAND AMERICA LINE

A Taste of
ELEGANCE
COOKBOOK

VOLUME II
Culinary Signature Collection

RUDI SODAMIN

RIZZOLI
NEW YORK

First published in the United States of America in 2008 by
Rizzoli International Publications, Inc.
300 Park Avenue South
New York, NY 10010
www.rizzoliusa.com

2008 2009 2010 2011 / 10 9 8 7 6 5 4 3 2 1

ISBN-13: 978-0-8478-2897-5

Library of Congress Control Number: 2008938013

Design: Susi Oberhelman

Printed in China

Page 1: Braised Short Ribs with Garlic Cloves and Baby Carrots (recipe page 122)
Page 2: Broiled Duck Breast with Thyme Sauce and Roasted Pears (recipe page 102)
Page 6: Grilled Vegetables with Red Bell Pepper Vinaigrette (recipe page 154)

DEDICATION

Magnus, Kenneth, and Kristina
There is no higher honor in the world than having the privilege of being your father.
No amount of money, no prestigious position I could ever attain,
or no item I could ever acquire would make me a richer man than I am.
You are precious beyond compare. You are the true treasure of my life.

CONTENTS

L I V I N G

Elegance is alive and well and circumnavigating the world aboard the ships of the Holland America Line. It is by design that we view elegance as a defining element of our company and a hallmark of our award-winning Signature of Excellence cruise experience. Holland America Line continues to enjoy an unrivaled reputation for providing our guests with "the kind of elegance that never goes out of style."

Therefore, it is with great pleasure that I welcome you to *Holland America Line Culinary Signature Collection Volume II: A Taste of Elegance* written by our own distinguished master chef—Rudi Sodamin. Over the course of his stellar career leading a revolution of culinary innovation in the cruise line industry, Master Chef Sodamin developed a philosophy by which any concept, word, person, or situation can be most clearly explained and understood by what he calls "Kitchen Wisdom."

"Cooking is the ultimate metaphor for everything in life," says Sodamin. "It's a universal language that everyone speaks." The ingredient list for Chef Sodamin's recipe for elegance includes grace, beauty, good taste, great style, and great quality.

At Holland America Line, these five ingredients are articulated in every detail, both large and small—from the stunning silhouette of our newest ship *Eurodam*, our first Signature-class vessel, to the flower arrangements that are carefully placed throughout each ship.

The intelligent cultivation of elegance is not about producing higher volume, but greater value. Holland America Line elegance never goes out of style because we consistently aim for excellence and to surpass our own benchmarks of success. Learning, refining, and rising to new challenges is what has made Holland America Line the undisputed leader in premium cruising.

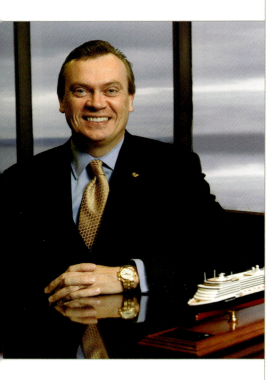

Stein Kruse, the president and Chief Executive Officer of Holland America Line, has overseen the building of the *Eurodam*, a mid-size ship with a 2,104-guest capacity.

ELEGANCE

Clearly, true elegance is not static, and it's never boring. As Master Chef Sodamin would say, something is always cooking. For example, when presented with the opportunity to create a culinary concept for Tamarind, a new pan-Asian restaurant on the *Eurodam*, Master Chef Sodamin enthusiastically whisked his legendary culinary creativity into high gear. He developed a sublime collection of Asian-inspired dishes and created a menu in which he categorized the entrées under the headings of "Water"; "Wood"; "Fire"; and "Earth." Our exclusive Tamarind restaurant received tremendous attention and acclaim for its originality, ambience, and yes, elegance. You will find some recipes from Tamarind in these pages.

Ultimately, the secret to elegance—whether for a cruise line or a dinner party at home—lies in the quality of each and every choice and the vision of the person or people behind the choices. Whether it's creating new itineraries, developing intriguing restaurant concepts, or finding new ways to provide superb service, at Holland America Line every decision is well considered and innovatively rendered by the members of our dedicated team to provide our guests with an unparalleled experience. In short, we make elegance exciting.

This book, the second volume in the Holland America Line Culinary Signature Collection, exists to bring you insight into the world of Holland America Line's culinary refinement. We hope that our recipes, the beautiful photography, and Master Chef Sodamin's kitchen wisdom will inspire your imagination, stimulate your senses and those of your guests, and transport the excitement of Holland America Line elegance right into your home.

STEIN KRUSE
President and Chief Executive Officer

Holland America Line provides guests with an experience that reflects the glamour and romance of the sea, and every detail is essential to creating this ambience.

A MASTER

Rosenthal china and fine silverware are used onboard Holland America Line ships.

When I was a young boy growing up in Austria, I spent countless hours at my mother's side in the kitchen. Memories of the aromas of her cooking warm me to this day. As I peered into pots simmering away on the old stove, a love of cooking began to bubble up within me. I doubt, however, that I could ever have imagined the life I was to lead once I left my small village.

I was passionate about cooking, and with that passion came ambition—great ambition. I wanted to travel the entire globe, see the world, extract every culinary secret. I wanted to become more than I was, to become more than I ever thought I could be. For many years, my goal was to learn as much as possible, and to reach the highest peaks of culinary achievement. And I did. I became—and remain—the most highly decorated chef at sea.

I had a meteoric rise in my career, attaining top-level culinary positions on famed cruise lines at a very young age. At twenty-three, I wrote my first cookbook and became the corporate executive chef of the Cunard Line. Somehow, I became a celebrity chef, before the term "celebrity chef" was even coined. I was invited to create menus and cook state dinners for dignitaries around the globe, including Her Royal Highness Queen Mother, Her Royal Highness Queen Elizabeth II, Princess Diana, Prince Charles, Israeli Prime Minister Shimon Perez, British Prime Minister Margaret Thatcher, President F. W. de Klerk of South Africa, Nelson Mandela, the Emperor of Japan and family, and President Bill Clinton, to drop but a few of the big names for whom I have cooked.

Praise in the media rolled in for my work (I was written up as "the Paul Bocuse of the Seven Seas"), and the walls of my dining room at home were filling with commendations, honors, awards, and letters of gratitude. I achieved great success and high notoriety, but, more importantly, over those years I learned much about myself and my potential, and I expanded my true professional aspirations.

For example, I learned that my passion for teaching and working with people in a team rivals that of my passion for culinary innovation

CHEF'S LIFE

and achieving culinary kudos. Inspiring young chefs and home cooks to keep learning about what can be done in a kitchen and how cooking is truly a brilliant and artistic form of self expression has given me great satisfaction and joy. Over the years, it has been my privilege to mentor many chefs rising through the ranks, as well as to work side by side with more seasoned chefs exchanging wild ideas, successful experiments, and stories from the sea so uncanny they have to be true.

Working in a galley kitchen is not an easy life, though. Down in the lower decks of ships, I've met the most dedicated, professional, and talented culinarians you could ever hope to meet. As long as the shifts are, as hard as the work is, these chefs and cooks thrive because of the passion they have for the work they do. The orchestral teamwork in a galley is the heart of providing excellent dining experiences.

Canaletto is one of the restaurants on the *Eurodam*. It is a casual Italian restaurant with a wonderful menu and wine list.

I also discovered while working on the corporate side of the cruise line business that leadership is leadership, be it in the galley or in the boardroom. As I developed leadership acumen on the corporate side, I discovered yet another passion. I immersed myself in the business of culinary operations for cruise lines. I studied how to get the best quality food product and how to locate and retain the most talented chefs in the world (in fact, I hired the first-ever female executive chefs for cruise lines). With the same passion, focus, and creativity I applied to creating menus, I created short- and long-range strategic plans to improve services, give passengers more, and make the experience more exciting, all while developing processes to stream-line operations, improve communications, and promote the cruise line. What a wonderful way to make a living!

I became very involved in the planning and design of the galley on new ships. I orchestrated the intense logistics for culinary operations for new vessel launches. And all of this innovation, cranking out new ideas, and working with teams to realize their visions were far lower in public profile than my culinary stardom. Yet, they proved just as exciting to me and gave me great insight into what the future of cruising could be and what a stupendous role the culinary aspect could play in the overall guest experience. I tell you, it was scintillating to be part of the driving force of it all, whether behind the scenes or center stage.

Over what now could arguably amount to a lifetime at sea, I've learned that the most important ingredients to a great culinary experience are in the hands of the crew and its management. I've come to realize that I love what I do, because it enables me to work with other passionate people, other innovative leaders, and provides an endless world of creative culinary opportunity to bring pleasure to people who appreciate a great dining experience.

Working as the master chef for Holland America Line allows me to take all my accumulated years of kitchen wisdom—my corporate boardroom leadership experience, my knowledge of how to inspire and manage staff, and, of course, my passion for culinary creativity—and put it all to good use.

It's like when I'm cooking at home in my kitchen or in our own Holland America Line R&D kitchen and nothing is wasted: egg whites get frozen for a future angel cake; crusts of bread are saved for croutons or bread pudding; saved oyster shells inspire a presentation

Eurodam's spectacular atrium features transparent flower-shaped forms that descend from the ceiling.

of escargot that will make anyone do a double-take before they can even lift a fork (see page 38 for recipe).

Working with Holland America Line is like that—none of my skills or my experience or talents are ever wasted. I am proud to have my golden signed master chefs hat toque emblazoned on all the menus, as well as proffer my master chef featured daily special.

Invariably, after I complete a cooking demonstration in the Culinary Arts Center, at least one student will linger after the demo, or a passenger on the ship will recognize me from a previous cruise and strike up a conversation. That person always has one burning question on his or her lips: "What does a consulting master chef do?"

It's not a simple question to answer, particularly for me. It is my nature, my temperament, my passion, if you will, to do things in new ways, to do things that have not been done before, or perhaps not even imagined before.

I'm frequently tempted to answer simply: "I cook up ideas."

It's short but true. A good example was when I created the "Going Wild on Wild Salmon" dinner for Holland America Line itineraries to

The *Eurodam* is Holland America Line's first Signature-class ship, representing the latest in technology and amenities.

Alaska, or when I proposed the master chef's dinner theme, a rather raucous, spectacular culinary evening where each of the thousand guests in the main dining room sport a white master chefs jacket and a toque just like mine. That one was a huge hit. So, a big part of my job is to take the ideas I come up with and present them to the Holland America Line Culinary Operations Team and then work with various teams, including the Entertainment Group, to make each happen.

While there are glamorous things I get to do in the course of my job as consulting master chef, such as hobnobbing with guests, speaking with the media, and developing special dinners for dignitaries and special events, my most important job for Holland America Line is working with the teams in the galley.

Quite honestly, it's where the hardest work happens, and where the training, the teamwork, and the culinary talent do the seemingly impossible: creating thousands of delicious, spectacular meals in the middle of the ocean. It takes hundreds of people and round-the-clock work in the galley.

Fostering a strong culinary team across the fleet, listening to the needs of knowledgeable chefs, and finding solutions to get those needs met is of prime importance to me, and, ultimately, to our guests. When

Tamarind is *Eurodam*'s pan-Asian restaurant, a new concept in onboard dining that gives guests even more options. The Silk Den lounge offers exotic cocktails in a romantic atmosphere.

The Culinary Arts Center presented by *Food & Wine* magazine has been a huge success onboard Holland America Line ships and continues on *Eurodam*.

I visit a beautiful ship in the Holland America Line fleet, I work side by side with the chefs as part of the culinary brigade. This enables me to observe, make recommendations, write a review of the galley perform-ance, and find ways to improve systems and protocols. I also introduce new dishes I've developed and demonstrate the presentation of them. Furthermore, the waitstaff is a critical part of the team, so it's important for me to offer motivational speeches and tips on new service trends to servers, busboys, headwaiters, and so on. The teaching, training, and team-building effort is an ongoing part of my job.

I travel from ship to ship to manage, advise, create, instruct, inspect, inspire, and offer guidance. I report back to the United States corporate headquarters in Seattle with recommendations on how to continue to elevate the efficiency and excellence of the Holland America Line culinary operations department, a massive undertaking! I make the recommendations, and then, as a team, we all go to work to fully articulate the idea and then implement it.

For example, early on in my tenure with Holland America Line, I saw a way to bring greater consistency to our already beautiful plate presentations. We reviewed each recipe, developed a presentation standard for it, and I took a picture of each one, the way I wanted to see it presented. When a dish is on the menu, an image of it is posted right on the wall of the galley, so the final presentation in the dining room is picture-perfect every time.

I find that as master chef of Holland America Line—a corporation so committed to providing its guests with experiences of culinary excellence and interest that it has a state-of-the-art Culinary Arts Center demonstration kitchen on each of its fourteen vessels, and has its own culinary training school in Manila—the more I do, the more I feel inspired to do.

The guests at Holland America Line are extremely engaged in all things culinary, and give us the most extraordinarily detailed feedback on their experiences. Guests' comments inform everything we do. They are the yardstick by which we measure our progress.

It's important to me to inspire guests to continue to enjoy their Holland America Line Signature of Excellence experience at home. Though I have previously published nine other cookbooks, being entrusted with writing the first cookbook in the 135-year history of Holland America Line was a great honor.

Now, I am equally excited to present this cookbook, the second installment of what has now become known as the "Holland America Line Culinary Signature Collection." Who knows down the line what else will be available for guests from the Signature Collection— naturally, I have some tasty ideas. Stay tuned.

Now, let's get cooking!
RUDI SODAMIN

Rudi Sodamin's Signature Base Plate

Flavor. Flavor. Flavor. | What is fine cooking about if not delivering great taste? Certainly cooking techniques such as roasting impart rich flavor to beef, fish, and even vegetables, but without pestos, salsas, herbed butters, and, of course, sauces, one dish of baked salmon would scarcely vary in flavor, texture, and color from another. | What you'll find in this chapter are ways to make even the simplest salad, meat, or poultry preparation into something exciting and memorable. And it couldn't be easier. With the notable exception of the delicious Sauce Béarnaise, every recipe here can be made at least a day ahead of time, and many of them even weeks. | Whenever I write a cookbook, I get most excited about producing this section, where I get to teach some techniques and give recipes that can be used over and over again to create hundreds of simple yet elegant meals. The recipes here bring additional layers of flavor, as well as color and texture variations to salads, pastas, simply cooked meats and poultry, fish, game—you name it. | While some of these recipes, which I call "pantry staples," are used in recipes in various chapters, like the Spicy Pear Salsa that accompanies the Grilled Strip Steak, the point of this section of the book is to give you easy access to these recipes to create your own dishes. Got some great pork chops? Try serving them with that same Spicy Pear Salsa. I recommend always having a compound butter like the Tarragon Butter on hand in the freezer. Unexpected guests coming over? No problem—grill up a quick steak and top it with a slice of Tarragon Butter, which will quickly melt making for a classic presentation and a delicious dish. | Use the recipes in this chapter to be ready for anything—especially adventures in dining!

SAUCES & DRESSINGS

Pestos

Pesto sauce originated in Liguria, Italy, and began as a flavoring for vegetable soups. Early versions consisted of an herb (basil, but sometimes parsley or marjoram instead) pounded and pressed by hand with a mortar and pestle and mixed with extra virgin olive oil, salt, and sometimes garlic. Pesto evolved to also include Parmesan and/or Pecorino cheese and pine nuts (or, in some regions, walnuts or hazelnuts). In the early twentieth century it began to be used as a sauce for pasta, after which, in more contemporary times, people began creating "pestos" made with other main ingredients, such as sun-dried tomatoes, chipotle or bell peppers, arugula, spinach, or mushrooms.

YIELD: APPROXIMATELY 2 CUPS

2 cups lightly packed basil leaves, preferably the smaller leaves from the top of the plant, rinsed and thoroughly dried in a salad spinner, then roughly chopped

2 to 4 medium cloves garlic, roughly chopped (remove any bitter green shoots from the middle and discard them)

¼ cup pine nuts or 3 tablespoons chopped walnuts

¼ teaspoon kosher salt

¼ cup extra virgin olive oil, divided

½ cup grated Parmesan cheese

BASIL PESTO

Basil pesto lends a savory edge when added to panini, dips, and barbecued meats. Spread on small toasted bread rounds and top with soft cheese and sliced tomato. Add to pasta salads or soups. Add lemon juice and more olive oil and toss with salads. Whisk into mayonnaise for a great sandwich spread or French fry dip. Mixed with fresh warm goat cheese, pesto makes an exciting dip or appetizer spread.

In a blender, combine the basil, garlic, nuts, salt, and half the olive oil. Blend, adding more olive oil, if necessary, to get the ingredients moving (you'll have to frequently stop to scrape down the sides). Once a paste forms, stir in the cheese and additional olive oil. (Alternatively, use a food processor: Combine the basil, garlic, and nuts. Pulse until well blended. Add the salt and cheese and pulse again. While the food processor is running, add the remaining olive oil in a steady stream until a thick, smooth paste forms.)

Accompanies Caesar Salad Bouquet (page 67)

STORING PESTO

Extra pesto stores in the refrigerator for at least a week. Pour a layer of olive oil on top and then cover in plastic wrap. Pesto can be frozen for up to 6 months, but it's best to freeze it without the cheese and then add the cheese after thawing.

SUN-DRIED TOMATO PESTO

Sun-dried tomatoes that aren't packed in oil are fresher tasting than those in oil, but choose moist-looking ones. This pesto makes a bright and lively sauce for grilled shrimp or grilled chicken tossed with pasta. Layer with cream cheese and basil pesto in a bowl as a spread for crackers and bread. Try on turkey sandwiches with havarti cheese, lettuce, and tomato.

In a skillet, bring the water to a simmer over medium heat. Add the tomatoes; as soon as the simmer returns, reduce the heat to medium-low. Cook, stirring, for 1 minute. Remove from the heat and let cool to room temperature.

 Combine the sun-dried tomatoes and their liquid, cheese, basil, pine nuts, and garlic in a food processor. Pulse until well blended. While the food processor is running, add oil in a steady stream until a thick, smooth paste is formed. (This pesto will keep, covered, in the refrigerator for up to 2 weeks.)

Accompanies Red Bell Peppers Stuffed with Barley (page 162)

YIELD: 2 CUPS

⅓ cup water

1 cup sun-dried tomatoes not packed in oil, chopped

½ cup grated Romano cheese or Parmesan cheese

¼ cup chopped fresh basil or 1 tablespoon dried basil

2 tablespoons pine nuts

2 medium cloves garlic

⅓ cup extra virgin olive oil, plus extra as needed

Classic Sauces

We use specific sauces to complement particular foods in order to bring balance of flavor and texture. The Basic Tomato Sauce and Quick Béarnaise Sauce recipes are just two of the many sauces to use for pasta and filet mignon, respectively, and these versions are just two of the many wonderful versions out there. I hope you enjoy them!

BASIC TOMATO SAUCE (Marinara)

YIELD: 4 SERVINGS

3 tablespoons pure olive oil

1 yellow onion, chopped

6 medium cloves garlic, very thinly sliced

½ teaspoon crushed red pepper

2 tablespoons good-quality tomato paste

1 (28-ounce) can Italian plum tomatoes, preferably San Marzano, chopped, juices reserved

1 (15-ounce) can good-quality canned tomato sauce

1 teaspoon sugar

1½ teaspoons dried basil, crumbled, or 1 tablespoon minced fresh basil

¾ teaspoon dried oregano, crumbled

2 bay leaves, preferably Turkish

Salt and freshly ground black pepper

A basic tomato sauce made with canned tomatoes bursts to life when you fold in chopped fresh tomatoes and basil right before serving. It produces fresh flavor yet saves you from having to peel and chop pounds and pounds of fresh tomatoes before you even start cooking. An alternative presentation (as shown in the photo, page 81) is to serve this dish deconstructed: Toss the hot pasta quickly with the fresh tomatoes, mozzarella, and basil and place it on a bed of basic tomato sauce, which allows you to mix the ingredients together with each forkful.

Heat the olive oil over medium heat in a large skillet. Add the onion and cook, stirring, until tender but not browned, about 10 minutes. Add the garlic and cook until it becomes a pale gold (do not let it brown), about 1 minute. Stir in the crushed red pepper and tomato paste and cook for 15 seconds. Add the chopped canned tomatoes and their reserved juices; cover, reduce the heat to low, and simmer, stirring once or twice, for 15 minutes. Add the tomato sauce, sugar, basil, oregano, and bay leaves. Cover and cook for 15 minutes longer. Uncover and simmer, stirring occasionally, until slightly thickened, about 5 minutes. Remove the bay leaves from the sauce.

If you'd like a smoother texture, transfer the sauce to a food processor or use a handheld stick blender. Season with salt and pepper. (The tomato sauce will keep, covered, in the refrigerator for up to 1 day or in the freezer for up to 1 month.)

Accompanies Penne with Tomato, Fresh Mozzarella, Basil, and Shaved Parmigiano-Reggiano (page 80)

QUICK BÉARNAISE SAUCE

In a blender, combine the egg yolks, salt, pepper, tarragon, and 1 table-spoon lemon juice. In a small saucepan, heat the butter until it melts and begins to foam.

Blend the egg yolk mixture at high speed for 2 to 3 seconds. Uncover the blender and, keeping a towel poised to catch any splatters, slowly add the hot butter in a very thin stream while blending at high speed until the mixture is thick (don't pour in any of the white milk solids at the bottom of the pan).

Adjust seasoning, adding more salt, pepper, or lemon juice if necessary. Use immediately, or store for up to 15 minutes in a bowl set in a larger bowl of tepid (but not warm) water.

Accompanies Filet Mignon and Shrimp "Land and Sea" (page 118)

YIELD: APPROXIMATELY 1 CUP

3 large egg yolks (see page 65 for information on using raw egg yolks)

¼ teaspoon salt

Pinch freshly ground black pepper

1 tablespoon chopped fresh tarragon or 1½ teaspoons dried tarragon

1 to 2 tablespoons fresh lemon juice

8 tablespoons (1 stick) butter, cut into small pieces

Compound Butters

Whenever you have leftover herbs in your refrigerator, there's no better use for them than compound butter. The butter will keep, well wrapped, in the refrigerator for up to 3 days and in the freezer, stored in an airtight plastic bag, for up to 6 weeks. Slices of compound butter are a fresh and lively topping for fish, meats, and vegetables. Several recipes follow, but feel free to improvise with whatever herbs or seasonings you have on hand.

TARRAGON BUTTER

YIELD: 6 SERVINGS

¼ cup dry white wine

1 tablespoon minced shallot

¼ teaspoon dried tarragon

5 tablespoons butter, at room temperature

1 tablespoon minced fresh tarragon

2 teaspoons fresh lemon juice

Sea salt and freshly ground black pepper

Add a slice or two of this butter on top of grilled steaks or lobster or even steamed potatoes or green beans.

Bring the wine, shallot, and dried tarragon to a boil in a small saucepan over medium-low heat until the liquid evaporates, about 2 minutes. Remove from the heat and cool completely.

In a small bowl, combine the butter, fresh tarragon, lemon juice, and shallot mixture. Use a rubber spatula to press and fold the ingredients together. Season with sea salt and pepper. Scrape the butter mixture onto a sheet of waxed paper and form into a log about 1½ inches in diameter. Roll in plastic wrap and chill in the refrigerator until firm, at least 2 hours.

Accompanies Filet Mignon and Shrimp "Land and Sea" (page 118)

BLUE CHEESE BUTTER

YIELD: 8 TO 10 SERVINGS

8 tablespoons (1 stick) butter, at room temperature

4 ounces crumbled Roquefort cheese (about 1 cup)

2 teaspoons minced chives or minced shallot

Sea salt and freshly ground black pepper

Add a slice of this butter on top of a grilled steak, or toss it with steamed vegetables, potatoes, or tofu. Variations include adding 2 teaspoons of Dijon mustard or substituting 2 tablespoons of port for the chives.

In a small bowl, combine the butter, cheese, and chives. Use a rubber spatula to press and fold the ingredients together. Season with sea salt and pepper. Scrape the mixture onto a sheet of waxed paper and form into a log about 1½ inches in diameter. Roll in plastic wrap and chill in the refrigerator until firm, at least 2 hours.

Accompanies Grilled Strip Steak (page 121)

CHIVE AND MIXED HERB BUTTER

This versatile compound butter can dress up fish, chicken, steak, rice, vegetables, or bread. Instead of using slices, you can grate the frozen butter with a cheese grater over fish, corn on the cob, or wherever you'd like a uniform distribution of flavor.

In a small bowl, combine the butter, chives, dill, thyme, and lemon juice. Use a rubber spatula to press and fold the ingredients together. Season with sea salt and pepper. Scrape the mixture onto a sheet of waxed paper and form into a log about 1½ inches in diameter. Roll in plastic wrap and chill in the refrigerator until firm, at least 2 hours.

Accompanies Butter-Basted Sole (page 142)

Accompanies Butter-Basted Sole (page 142)

YIELD: 8 SERVINGS

8 tablespoons (1 stick) butter, at room temperature

2 tablespoons chopped fresh chives

1 tablespoon chopped fresh dill

1 tablespoon chopped fresh thyme

1 tablespoon fresh lemon juice

Sea salt and freshly ground black pepper

Salsas

A salsa is comprised of raw, cooked, or partially cooked ingredients brought together in such a way so that the overall flavor is harmonious even though each component can be tasted distinctly. Flavors and textures are meant to stand out in salsas, unlike in traditional sauces where cooking produces a more homogenous experience. Because of their fresh nature, salsas are best eaten the same day they're made.

SPICY PEAR SALSA

YIELD: APPROXIMATELY 3 CUPS

2 firm but ripe Anjou or Bosc pears (about 1¼ pounds total), peeled, cored, and cut into ½-inch cubes

½ cup finely chopped red onion

¼ cup (about 2 medium) jalapeño, deseeded, deveined, and finely chopped

3 tablespoons fresh lemon juice

3 tablespoons extra virgin olive oil

Sea salt and freshly ground black pepper

½ cup coarsely chopped fresh cilantro

Cut the preparation time by substituting drained canned pears for fresh.

In a medium glass or ceramic bowl, combine all the ingredients except for the cilantro and let stand at room temperature for 1 hour. Season with sea salt and pepper. Stir in the cilantro and serve immediately.

Accompanies Grilled Strip Steak (page 121)

TROPICAL FRUIT SALSA

YIELD: 2½ CUPS

¼ cup peeled, chopped pineapple

¼ cup finely chopped mango

¼ cup seeded and finely diced papaya

Zest and juice of 1 lime

1 medium jalapeño, deseeded, deveined, and finely chopped

1 red bell pepper, seeded and diced

¼ cup chopped scallions

1 teaspoon kosher salt

2 tablespoons chopped cilantro

Any leftover salsa makes a terrific marinade for grilled shrimp.

In a medium glass or ceramic bowl, combine all the ingredients except the cilantro and let stand at room temperature for 1 hour. Stir in the cilantro and serve immediately.

YIELD: 1½ CUPS

1 ripe mango, diced

1 small red onion, diced

½ red bell pepper, cored, seeded, and diced

3 tablespoons fresh lime juice

1 small green chile, such as a serrano, thinly sliced

3 tablespoons finely chopped cilantro

Salt and freshly ground black pepper

MANGO AND RED BELL PEPPER SALSA

This delicious salsa pairs beautifully with fish preparations, including grilled fish, and with its bright colors—the orange mango and red bell pepper—it looks lovely too.

In a medium glass or ceramic bowl, combine all the ingredients except for the cilantro and let stand at room temperature for 1 hour. Season with salt and pepper. Stir in the cilantro and serve immediately.

Accompanies Coconut Seared Scallops (page 151)

YIELD: 1½ CUPS

4 medium tomatoes, seeded and diced (see page 70)

1 small red onion, finely chopped

2 serrano chiles or jalapeños, deseeded, deveined, and finely chopped

2 tablespoons chopped fresh cilantro

½ teaspoon salt

Pinch of freshly ground black pepper

1 to 2 tablespoons fresh lime juice

TOMATO SALSA

A classic tomato salsa is easy to make and tasty, and it spices up any party—just add an assortment of tortilla chips.

In a glass or ceramic bowl, combine the tomatoes, onion, chiles, cilantro, salt, and pepper. Stir and toss well. Season with lime juice. Let the salsa stand for 30 minutes before serving. (The salsa keeps, tightly covered, in the refrigerator for up to 2 days.)

Mayonnaise

A mayonnaise is basically a vinaigrette stabilized with egg yolk. Homemade mayonnaise is much more flavorful than store-bought, and can be enhanced with any number of flavorings. Puréed roasted garlic, curry powder, roasted red bell pepper, chipotle, and minced herbs are just a few possibilities.

BASIC MAYONNAISE

Matching a freshly made mayonnaise with fresh ingredients makes all the difference in sandwiches and salads.

Combine the egg yolks and mustard in a food processor. Blend until smooth. Season with salt, white pepper, and Worcestershire sauce. With the motor running, add the olive oil in a slow, steady stream through the feed tube, stopping once or twice to scrape down the sides. The mixture should become very thick. Add the lemon juice and blend until incorporated. Adjust the seasonings and transfer to a container. Cover and refrigerate until ready to use. (Fresh mayonnaise can be stored, covered, in the refrigerator for up to 4 days.)

YIELD: 1 ½ CUPS

2 large egg yolks (see page 65 for information about raw eggs)

1 teaspoon Dijon mustard

Salt and freshly ground white pepper

Worcestershire sauce

1½ cups extra virgin olive oil

1 tablespoon fresh lemon juice

Hors d'oeuvres and canapés being served on a Holland America Line cruise must be nothing short of spectacular every time, all the time. | In the galley we have a class of recipes that our chefs refer to as the "cocktail appetizer" collection. These are exceptional little dishes, each featuring a luxury indulgence ingredient—caviar, duck liver, escargot, and the like. | The cocktail appetizer recipes included here are for those super-important occasions—when there's something or someone to celebrate, or simply a party from which you want your friends to walk away saying, "the food was to die for!" These small bites are for sky's-the-limit entertaining. | Food should always present a feast for the eyes, mind, and palate. Never, however, is this more critical than for the very first tastes that greet the guests. Each of these recipes meets that important requirement, yet none are hard to duplicate. The six canapés *look* impressive but are truly easy to make; they simply require a bit of assembly work at the end—the details of which are fully articulated in these pages. | Other recipes in this section are Holland America Line all-time favorites: Shrimp Cocktail with Cocktail Sauce, Tapenade Toasts, and Tomato and Goat Cheese Tartlets. You'll also find a new favorite directly from the menu at Holland America Line's new pan-Asian restaurant Tamarind: Tamarind's Satay Skewers with Spicy Peanut Dipping Sauce. | Make one or make many, you can mix and match any of these small bites to serve prior to any style main course, or have a true cocktail party and make them all, omitting a main course entirely!

CHAPTER 2

SMALL BITES

Canapés

With these six recipes you can use favorite ingredients such as shrimp, smoked salmon, prosciutto, and Gorgonzola cheese to create elegant, tasty, and unique finger foods that will be perfect for your next dinner party. While the presentation looks fancy and will certainly impress your guests, they are easy to make.

10 jumbo shrimp, cooked

1½ teaspoons fresh lemon juice

Pinch cayenne pepper

10 rounds three-grain bread, toasted until golden brown

10 small pieces red oak lettuce

10 red grapes

¼ cup cocktail sauce

JUMBO SHRIMP ON THREE-GRAIN BREAD CROUTON

Combine the shrimp, lemon juice, and cayenne pepper in a glass bowl. Allow to marinate, covered, in the refrigerator for 2 hours.

To serve, top a bread crouton with a piece of lettuce. Toss the shrimp with the sauce in a bowl; use a toothpick to secure a shrimp and grape to the crouton. Serve immediately.

COOKING SHRIMP

To cook shrimp, buy shell-on large shrimp (they can be purchased deveined) and add them to a pot of boiling salted water. Cook, stirring occasionally, for 2 to 3 minutes, until the shrimp is no longer raw in the middle (test by cutting into 1 shrimp after 2 minutes). Don't overcook. Remove the shrimp and plunge into ice water to stop the cooking. Drain immediately. Peel—leaving the tail shells on if you wish—and reserve, covered in the refrigerator, until ready to serve.

10 rounds white bread, toasted until golden brown

10 small pieces Boston (Bibb) lettuce or leaf lettuce

5 ounces store-bought duck liver pâté, well chilled and cut into 10 slices

5 segments orange, membranes removed and segments cut in half

2 tablespoons lingonberry preserves

DUCK LIVER MOUSSE AND LINGONBERRY COMPOTE

Top each piece of toasted bread with a piece of lettuce followed by a slice of pâté and half an orange segment. Spoon ½ teaspoon of lingonberry preserves on the canapé and serve immediately.

SMOKED SALMON ROSETTE ON PUMPERNICKEL BREAD

YIELD: 10 SERVINGS

3 tablespoons crème fraîche

1 tablespoon peeled, seeded, and minced cucumber

2 teaspoons minced dill plus 10 small sprigs dill (for garnish)

10 (1-inch) squares pumpernickel bread

2 tablespoons cream cheese, softened

10 small pieces Boston lettuce

10 ounces sliced smoked salmon, rolled into 10 rosettes (or used flat)

10 small capers (for garnish)

In a small bowl, combine the crème fraîche, cucumber, and minced dill. Set aside.

Lightly spread each pumpernickel square with the cream cheese and top with a piece of lettuce and salmon. Spoon some of the cucumber mixture onto the top of the salmon. Garnish with a dill sprig and caper and serve immediately.

PROSCIUTTO-WRAPPED WATERMELON ON CANTALOUPE

YIELD: 10 SERVINGS

¼ cup sugar

¼ cup water

Juice of 2 limes

Pinch crushed red pepper

1 teaspoon chopped mint leaves plus 10 mint leaves (for garnish)

10 (½-inch) balls seedless watermelon

10 (½-inch) cubes cantaloupe

10 small strips prosciutto

10 small strawberry wedges

In a heavy 1-quart saucepan, combine the sugar and water. Bring to a boil, stirring to dissolve the sugar. Boil for 1 minute (do not let the syrup become brown while boiling). Remove from the heat and let cool.

Measure out ¼ cup sugar syrup and pour it into a glass or ceramic bowl (discard any remaining syrup). Stir in the lime juice, crushed red pepper, and chopped mint. Add the watermelon and cantaloupe, and gently toss to coat. Allow to marinate, covered, in the refrigerator for 3 hours, stirring occasionally.

To serve, drain the fruit. Wrap each watermelon ball with a strip of prosciutto and place it on top of a piece of cantaloupe. Garnish with mint leaves and strawberry wedges and serve immediately.

BLUE CHEESE SWIRL WITH ORANGE

In a medium bowl, use a hand mixer to beat the Gorgonzola until creamy and smooth. Add the cream and beat just until fluffy (do not overbeat). Transfer the cheese mixture to a pastry bag fitted with a star tip.

Top each bread crouton with a lettuce leaf. Pipe a rosette of cheese onto the lettuce. Place a parsley sprig, orange segment, and walnut half on the canapé and serve immediately.

YIELD: 10 SERVINGS

5 ounces Gorgonzola cheese, crumbled

¼ cup heavy cream

10 rounds whole-wheat bread, toasted until golden brown

10 pieces red oak lettuce

10 sprigs parsley

10 mandarin orange segments

10 small walnut halves, toasted

BAY SHRIMP "CEVICHE" IN BOUCHÉES

In a glass or ceramic bowl, combine the shrimp, coconut cream, lime juice, red bell pepper, red onion, jalapeño, cilantro, and cayenne. Allow to marinate, covered, in the refrigerator for 2 hours.

To serve, scoop the shrimp mixture into the baked puff pastry shells. Garnish with the tomato wedges and serve immediately.

YIELD: 10 SERVINGS

10 ounces cooked bay shrimp, rinsed

2 tablespoons canned coconut cream

Juice of 2 limes

2 tablespoons minced jarred red bell pepper

2 tablespoons minced red onion

1 medium jalapeño, deseeded, deveined, and minced

1 tablespoon minced fresh cilantro leaves

Pinch cayenne pepper

10 store-bought puff pastry mini-shells, baked according to manufacturer's instructions

2 cherry tomatoes, each cut into 5 wedges (for garnish)

Grilled Asparagus and Bread with Parmigiano-Reggiano

YIELD: 4 SERVINGS

BALSAMIC VINAIGRETTE

2 tablespoons balsamic vinegar

1 tablespoon fresh lemon juice

¼ teaspoon Dijon mustard

½ cup extra virgin olive oil

Salt and freshly ground black pepper

ASPARAGUS AND CROUTONS

12 spears jumbo asparagus, tough ends peeled if necessary

4 tablespoons extra virgin olive oil, divided

1 tablespoon minced garlic plus 2 whole garlic cloves, halved

Sea salt and freshly ground black pepper

1 loaf sourdough baguette, about 20 inches long, cut into 8 or 12 diagonal slices (about 6 inches long)

4 ounces Parmigiano-Reggiano cheese, in one piece

¼ cup chopped chives

Pencil thin asparagus are too delicate for grilling. I use jumbo asparagus because they stand up to the grill and you can sink your teeth into their deliciousness. If the bottom inch or twoof the root end of your asparagus has a tough outer layer, remove it with a vegetable peeler. This allows the entire spear to cook evenly from end to end.

BALSAMIC VINAIGRETTE

In a glass or stainless steel bowl, combine the vinegar, lemon juice, and mustard. Slowly whisk in the olive oil. Season with salt and pepper. Cover and refrigerate until ready to use.

ASPARAGUS AND CROUTONS

Heat a grill (charcoal, gas, or electric) to medium hot (when you can hold your hand 5 inches above the rack for 3 to 4 seconds). In a large mixing bowl, combine the asparagus, 2 tablespoons olive oil, and minced garlic. Season with sea salt (crushed with a rolling pin if it's very coarse).

Grill the asparagus and bread slices on a lightly oiled grill rack until well marked but not burned, 4 minutes on each side for the asparagus and 1 to 2 minutes total for the bread. Return the asparagus to the mixing bowl and toss with any oil remaining in the bowl. Immediately rub 1 side of each bread slice with the cut side of a garlic half. Brush the bread with the remaining 2 tablespoons olive oil and sprinkle with sea salt. (Alternatively, grill the asparagus and bread in a hot, lightly oiled ridged grill pan over moderately high heat.)

Divide the asparagus and bread slices among 4 plates. Add shavings of Parmigiano-Reggiano, chives, and freshly ground black pepper. Drizzle each plate with 1 to 2 tablespoons of the balsamic vinaigrette.

Shrimp Cocktail with Cocktail Sauce

A traditional cocktail party staple is given a new life through its artful presentation and zesty sauce.

In a small glass or ceramic bowl, combine the ketchup, chili sauce, horseradish, lemon juice, scallions, Worcestershire sauce, and hot pepper sauce. Stir until combined. Cover and refrigerate until ready to use.

To serve, place some coleslaw mix in the bottom of 4 large martini glasses. Spoon some cocktail sauce on top and hang the shrimp over the rim. Garnish with the endive leaves, parsley, chive, and lemon wedges, and serve immediately.

YIELD: 4 SERVINGS

½ cup ketchup

¼ cup chili sauce

2 tablespoons horseradish, preferably freshly grated

2 tablespoons fresh lemon juice

2 teaspoons minced scallions, green parts only

½ teaspoon Worcestershire sauce

Hot pepper sauce, such as Tabasco

½ cup shredded carrot and coleslaw mix (without dressing)

1 pound large shrimp, peeled, deveined, cooked, and chilled

12 baby endive leaves, red and green (for garnish)

4 sprigs parsley (for garnish)

4 strands chive (for garnish)

1 lemon, cut into wedges (for garnish)

Escargots Baked in Oyster Shells

YIELD: 4 SERVINGS

1 (7- to-8-ounce) can escargots (about 16 to 24), drained and rinsed (you can find at specialty food markets or online)

2 tablespoons dry white wine, such as Sauvignon Blanc, Chenin Blanc, or Pinot Blanc

8 tablespoons (1 stick) butter, softened

1 tablespoon minced garlic

2 tablespoons finely chopped fresh flat-leaf parsley

1 tablespoon minced shallot

1 teaspoon Pernod or brandy (optional)

2 teaspoons coarse sea salt or artisan sea salt

Freshly ground black pepper

2 cups kosher salt (for stabilizing the oyster shells)

12 oyster shells, sterilized

¼ cup wakame seaweed, cut into very thin strips with kitchen shears and soaked in water for 30 minutes (optional)

1 crusty baguette, sliced (for dipping)

Next time you fry oysters or make an oyster stuffing, save the shells, run them through a hot dishwasher, and then bake them on a rack in the oven to sterilize them. They'll make a gorgeous and surprising presentation for escargots. Alternatively, serve the escargots in large fresh mushroom caps (prebake the caps in muffin tins for five minutes before filling). Whichever way you choose, don't forget to serve champagne!

Heat the oven to 400°F. Combine the escargots and wine in a small saucepan. Bring to a simmer over medium heat. When the escargots have absorbed all the wine, remove from the heat and let cool. Reserve.

In a food processor, purée the butter, garlic, parsley, shallot, and Pernod, if using. Season with some of the sea salt (more will be sprinkled on after baking) and pepper.

Pour the kosher salt into a large shallow baking pan and nestle the oyster shells in the salt. Divide half the flavored butter among the shells. Divide the reserved escargots among the shells and top with the seaweed, if using, and the remaining flavored butter.

Bake the escargots for 10 minutes, or until bubbling. Remove from the oven and sprinkle with more sea salt. Transfer the shells to serving plates, nestling them in more salt if you wish, and serve immediately with baguette slices.

HANDCRAFTED SALT

If you like to use salt, now is the time to try handcrafted varieties. Interest in salt has soared and salts from around the world are more readily available. Salts that are harvested and processed by hand bear distinctive nuances of flavor that add intrigue to simple fish or meat dishes. Whether pink, red, black, gray, or white (or even smoked or vanilla flavored!), most handcrafted salts bring out the best in food when sprinkled on after cooking.

Asian Pickled Vegetables

YIELD: 4 TO 6 SERVINGS

½ cup unseasoned rice vinegar

¼ cup sugar

1 teaspoon salt

2 medium carrots, cut into 2-inch-long matchsticks

½ hothouse (seedless) cucumber, peeled and cut into 2-inch-long matchsticks

½ cup thinly sliced red onion

These bright and crisp vegetables set off any sandwich and make a cooling accompaniment to our Satay Skewers (see page 42). If you have an adjustable blade slicer, all the easier, though a simple Y peeler can get you started with thin slices you can cut into matchsticks. To cut down on slicing time, you can also just substitute preshredded broccoli slaw for the carrots and cucumber.

In a glass or ceramic bowl, whisk together the vinegar, sugar, and salt. Add the carrots, cucumber, and onion, and stir to combine. Let stand, stirring occasionally, until wilted, about 15 minutes.

Tomato and Goat Cheese Tartlets

YIELD: 10 (2-INCH) TARTLETS

3 plum tomatoes

2 teaspoons herbes de Provence

Salt

Extra virgin olive oil, for drizzling

1 sheet frozen puff pastry (half of a 17.3-ounce package), thawed according to package instructions

2 ounces goat cheese, crumbled

Store-bought puff pastry can be used in so many savory and sweet preparations and it is always a favorite. Here it becomes the base for a delicious, very French combination of tomatoes, goat cheese, and herbes de Provence.

Heat the oven to 350°F. Slice the tomatoes into halves and place cut-side up on a baking sheet. Sprinkle with the herbes de Provence and season with salt. Drizzle with the olive oil and bake for 20 minutes. Remove from the oven and allow to cool.

Increase the oven temperature to 400°F. Chop the cooled tomatoes into ½-inch cubes.

Line a baking sheet with parchment paper. With a cookie cutter, cut 10 two-inch rounds of puff pastry. Place the puff pastry rounds on the prepared baking sheet and top with the chopped tomatoes. Sprinkle the goat cheese on top and bake for 10 minutes, or until the pastry is golden on the bottom.

Tapenade Toasts

YIELD: 20 SMALL TOASTS

Depending on the size of the bread used, these toasts can be part of a finger-food assortment (often called crostini) or meal-size open-face sandwiches that would be perfect with a salad. The smaller size would be particularly appealing on a tray with other toasts spread with egg salad and garlicky white-bean purée (use your favorite recipes). Look no farther than your pantry or refrigerator for inspiration.

Heat the oven to 375°F. In a food processor, finely chop the olives, capers, anchovies, and garlic. With the processor running, add ¼ cup olive oil in a steady stream until blended. Reserve.

Brush the bread slices with the remaining olive oil and arrange them on a baking sheet. Bake until golden, 10 to 12 minutes. Remove from the oven and let cool to room temperature.

Right before serving, spread the tapenade over the bread slices. If desired, garnish with the red bell pepper strips and sprinkle with the crumbled feta.

½ cup pitted kalamata olives

2 tablespoons drained bottled capers

2 canned anchovy fillets or 1 teaspoon anchovy paste

2 medium cloves garlic

¼ cup extra virgin olive oil plus ¼ cup extra for brushing on bread slices

20 slices of baguette or country-style Italian bread (sliced thinly at a 45-degree angle)

3 roasted red bell peppers (home-roasted or bottled), cut into thin strips (for garnish)

3 tablespoons crumbled feta cheese (for garnish)

HERBES DE PROVENCE

This mixture originating in southern France, consists of dried herbs used to season chicken, vegetables, and meat. It can be found in many supermarkets and may include such herbs and spices as rosemary, fennel seed, thyme, summer savory, basil, tarragon, lavender, chervil, marjoram, sage, bay leaves, cloves, and orange zest.

Tamarind's Satay Skewers with Spicy Peanut Dipping Sauce

A t Tamarind, our new pan-Asian restaurant onboard the *Eurodam*, we serve a satay sampler that includes lamb, beef, chicken, pork, and shrimp, each with different marinades. To make things easier, you can use the same marinade for three different skewers and serve them with a single delicious dipping sauce. As a cooling accompaniment, try the Asian Pickled Vegetables (see page 40).

YIELD: 12 SERVINGS

SPICY PEANUT DIPPING SAUCE

¾ cup unsalted peanuts

1 tablespoon granulated sugar

2 tablespoons peanut oil

1 tablespoon red curry paste

1½ cups unsweetened coconut milk

1 tablespoon soy sauce

1½ tablespoons fresh lime juice

SATAY SKEWERS

36 (6- or 8-inch) bamboo skewers

1¼ cups soy sauce

¼ cup red curry paste

¼ cup minced garlic

⅓ cup fresh lime juice

2¼ teaspoons ground coriander

¾ cup peanut oil

¾ cup honey

1 pound boneless sirloin or flank steak

1 pound boneless, skinless chicken breasts, well trimmed, cut lengthwise into ½-inch-wide strips

1 pound peeled and deveined medium shrimp

SPICY PEANUT DIPPING SAUCE

Place the peanuts and sugar in the bowl of a food processor and pulse until finely chopped.

Heat the peanut oil over medium heat in a medium saucepan. Whisk the curry paste and coconut milk into the peanut oil. Stir in the peanut mixture. Bring to a boil, stirring constantly. Remove from the heat and allow to cool slightly.

Pour the mixture back into the food processor and blend until smooth. If not using immediately, cover tightly and refrigerate. Just prior to serving, stir in the soy sauce and lime juice.

SATAY SKEWERS

Soak the skewers in water for 30 minutes. In a large glass or ceramic bowl, combine the remaining ingredients except for the steak, chicken, and shrimp. Whisk until smooth.

Trim and discard any excess fat from the steak. With a meat mallet or small heavy pot, pound the steak to a ¼-inch thickness. Slice the steak into ¾-inch strips, about 3 inches long.

Place the steak strips, chicken strips, and shrimp in a shallow glass or ceramic dish. Pour the marinade over, remove any air, and seal. Refrigerate and let marinate for up to 2 hours.

Preheat a grill or broiler on high. Thread steak, chicken, and shrimp separately onto bamboo skewers and grill for 1 to 3 minutes per side, or until just cooked through. (Alternatively, you can cook the satays in a hot, ridged grill pan over moderately high heat.) Serve hot or at room temperature with the dipping sauce.

Scrambled Eggs with Sour Cream and Caviar

YIELD: 4 SERVINGS

4 eggs

¼ cup sour cream

1½ teaspoons minced onion

Salt and freshly ground black pepper

1 tablespoon butter

1 (30-gram) jar American white sturgeon caviar (about 1 ounce)

4 fresh chive strands

Twenty years ago, when I was executive chef of the Cunard Line, we'd make three thousand of these eggs at a time for the QEII! These eggs are indeed easy and elegant. Serve with grilled, sliced bread or toast points.

With an egg topper, small pointed scissors, or a knife remove the top ½ inch of shell from the smaller tapered end of each egg. (Alternatively, gently press a hole into the egg with the wide end of a metal pastry tip.) Pour the contents into a medium bowl and set eggs aside (bits of shell may find their way into the eggs; they will be strained out later). Reserve the empty shells but discard the top caps.

Bring a medium pan of water to a boil. Add the egg shells and use a large flat spatula to gently hold the egg shells under the level of water to keep them submerged. Boil for 3 minutes. With a slotted spoon, remove the egg shells from the water and set them upside down on paper towels to dry (or, drain the egg shells on a paper towel placed over an empty egg carton).

In a small bowl, whisk the sour cream and onion. Season with salt (keeping in mind that the caviar will add saltiness) and pepper. Cover the bowl; refrigerate until needed.

When the egg shells are thoroughly dried, remove any fine white membrane from inside each egg shell, taking care not to break the shell. Set aside.

With a whisk or a stick blender, beat the eggs thoroughly until smooth, about 30 seconds. Strain the eggs through a medium sieve to remove any stray bits of shell.

In a small skillet, heat the butter over medium heat until melted and foamy white. Add the eggs and whisk constantly, drawing the whisk across the skillet and moving the skillet on and off the heat as necessary to avoid overcooking. Before they are fully cooked, remove the eggs from the skillet. Season with salt and pepper.

To serve, use a small spoon (or a pastry bag) to fill the prepared egg shells with some of the sour cream mixture. Spoon in the warm eggs to within ¼ inch of the top. Add another layer of the sour cream mixture and top with the caviar. Place the eggs in 4 egg cups, garnish with a chive strand, and serve immediately.

CAVIAR

Farm raised in California, American white sturgeon caviar is similar in quality and flavor to the Caspian sevruga caviar. Alternatively, you can use salmon roe or paddlefish caviar, or a combination of all three for an over-the-top presentation.

I cannot say enough about the pleasures of good soup. I grew up eating Hungarian soup; to this day, to think of it is to want a big steaming bowl. Of course in our home, soup and a hunk of bread was the entire meal. │ It was when I was a young chef working on cruise lines that I first encountered soup as anything but the main course. A first course of soup was de rigueur—an expectation on the luxury liners. I also had my first encounter with cold soup: in those days on cruise lines it was common practice to serve a chilled consommé. I was deeply suspicious of the concept of "cold" soup; if it wasn't hot, it wasn't soup. │ But as I traveled the globe, I encountered countless delicious soups that were served either at room temperature or chilled. I found these soups so dynamic and refreshing, they've become favorite inspirations. │ Here you will find hot and cold soups from Holland America Line menus. Our soups are beloved by our guests, and we frequently receive requests for the recipes shared here. │ Soup can be the most humble of dishes, but well-made and well-presented it brings an elegant touch of luxury to any meal. There is nothing magical about making great soup, hot or cold—all you need is a good recipe and quality ingredients. Ideal for serving at an elegant dinner party, each of the soup recipes in this section are easy to make and all can be made a day ahead. │ A lovely soup in a simple white bowl accented with one of the ingredients as a garnish is timelessly beautiful. Or, drop the bowl entirely and serve soup in a delicate demitasse as an appetizer. There's no rule that says guests must be seated to eat soup—in fact, Holland America Line has a century-old tradition of serving hot bouillon to stargazers at 11 p.m. Go ahead, start with the soup, add a dash of bold creativity and inaugurate new entertaining traditions in your home.

CHAPTER 3

SOUPS

Chilled Summer Gazpacho with Shrimp and Basil

Allowing the gazpacho ingredients to marinate together overnight before puréeing reduces the acidity and allows the flavors to blend.

GAZPACHO

In a large glass or ceramic bowl, combine all of the ingredients except for the salt and pepper. Allow to marinate in the refrigerator overnight.

The next day, purée the gazpacho ingredients in a blender in batches until smooth. (Alternatively, you can use a handheld stick blender, which will allow you to maintain a chunky texture, if you wish.) Season with salt and pepper.

SHRIMP AND FRIED BASIL LEAF GARNISH

Gently rinse and thoroughly dry the basil leaves (placing them on a kitchen towel in front of a fan will get them drier than a salad spinner).

In a 10- or 12-inch frying pan or cast-iron skillet, heat the vegetable oil over medium-high heat until a deep-frying thermometer registers 350°F (do not allow the oil to smoke). Line a baking sheet with sheets of paper towels.

When the oil is ready, add a handful of the basil leaves, being careful not to overcrowd the pan. Fry for 2 to 3 seconds, until they turn a brilliant green and are crisp. With a slotted spoon, carefully transfer the basil leaves to the prepared baking sheet. (Fried basil leaves should be used quickly or else they will lose their crispness.)

To serve, divide the soup among chilled soup bowls. Top with a whole shrimp and a fried basil leaf.

YIELD: 10 TO 12 SERVINGS

GAZPACHO

8 large vine-ripened tomatoes, cored, seeded, and quartered

1 large cucumber, seeded (peeling is optional)

1 medium red bell pepper, cored, seeded, and diced

1 medium green bell pepper, cored, seeded, and diced

1 medium jalapeño, deseeded, deveined, and diced

½ medium red onion, diced

3 medium cloves garlic, smashed

1 bunch (6 ounces) basil, leaves only

1 bunch (3 ounces) cilantro, leaves only

1 tablespoon ground cumin

⅛ cup sherry vinegar

¼ cup extra virgin olive oil

¼ loaf Italian bread (about ¼ pound), crust removed and diced

5 shakes Tabasco sauce

Juice of 2 limes

Salt and freshly ground black pepper

SHRIMP AND FRIED BASIL LEAF GARNISH

12 large fresh basil leaves

2 cups vegetable oil, for deep-frying

12 cooked jumbo shrimp (about ¾ pound), peeled

Chilled Cucumber Soup

YIELD: 6 TO 8 SERVINGS

2½ cups plain yogurt

½ cup store-bought vegetable stock

½ cup chopped fresh flat-leaf parsley

½ cup chopped fresh dill

1 tablespoon extra virgin olive oil

2 teaspoons minced garlic

Dash of Pernod, ouzo, sambuca, or anisette

4 medium cucumbers, peeled, seeded, and chopped plus 1 cucumber finely chopped (for garnish)

Salt and freshly ground white pepper

Sour cream and dill sprigs (for garnish)

I f you don't want to use any liqueur in this soup but still want the subtle licorice undertone, substitute chopped fresh fennel fronds for half of the chopped fresh dill.

In a blender or food processor, combine the yogurt, vegetable stock, parsley, dill, olive oil, garlic, and Pernod. Purée until smooth. Add the 4 chopped cucumbers and purée until very smooth and creamy. Season with salt and white pepper.

Transfer the soup to a clean glass or ceramic bowl. Cover and refrigerate until cold. To serve, divide the soup among chilled soup bowls and garnish with the reserved chopped cucumber, sour cream, and dill sprigs.

Mixed Berry Soup

ith its refreshing pop of berry flavor, this cold soup is like summer in bowl, but it can be enjoyed year-round if you use frozen raspberries.

Combine the sugar and water in a medium saucepan. Cook, stirring, over medium-high heat until the sugar is completely dissolved. Once the sugar is dissolved, stop stirring and bring the syrup to a boil.

Boil the syrup for 1 minute. Remove from the heat and let the syrup cool completely.

In a food processor, combine the raspberries, sugar syrup, and lemon juice. Process until smooth. Transfer the mixture to a fine-mesh sieve over a bowl and use a rubber spatula or a ladle to push it through to strain out the seeds. Cover the bowl and chill in the refrigerator until cold.

To serve, ladle the soup into chilled soup bowls. Top with the whole fruits. Garnish with the lemon balm and lemon zest, and serve immediately.

YIELD: 4 SERVINGS

1½ cups sugar

1¼ cups water

1½ cups fresh or frozen raspberries, thawed

1 tablespoon fresh lemon juice

1 cup any combination of fruits (blueberries, blackberries, halved and pitted cherries, raspberries, quartered strawberries, red currants)

Fresh lemon balm sprigs (for garnish)

Lemon zest, thinly sliced (for garnish)

Chilled Banana and Coconut Soup

YIELD: 5 SERVINGS

2 pounds ripe bananas, peeled and diced

2 cups canned coconut milk

2 cups lowfat vanilla frozen yogurt

½ cup pineapple juice

¼ cup dark rum or triple sec (optional)

Juice of 1 lemon

¼ cup sliced almonds

 smooth and creamy combination of bananas and coconut milk is given a hint of crunch with a toasted almond garnish.

In a large glass or ceramic bowl, combine all of the ingredients except for the almonds. Ladle the mixture in batches into a blender and purée until smooth. Transfer the soup to a clean glass or ceramic bowl. Cover and refrigerate until cold.

Meanwhile, toast the almonds: In a dry heavy skillet over medium-high heat, toss or stir the almonds, until lightly browned, 3 to 4 minutes; take care not to scorch them. To serve, divide the cold soup among chilled soup bowls and garnish with the almonds.

Corn and Yellow Squash Soup with Crabmeat

T o make even mounds of crab in the soup bowls, place a two-inch ring mold or biscuit cutter in the bowl and press the crab mixture gently into it. Remove the mold and pour the soup around the mound of crab.

CORN AND SQUASH SOUP

In a large saucepan heat the butter over medium heat. Add the leek and onions and cook, stirring, until the vegetables soften and become translucent, about 5 minutes (the vegetables should not brown). Add the garlic, corn, and squash and cook, stirring, for 2 minutes more.

Add the sage, chipotle powder, and chicken stock, and bring to a boil. Reduce the heat to low and simmer, stirring occasionally, about 8 minutes. Add the cream and cook for 3 minutes more. Remove from the heat and let cool for 10 minutes.

Transfer the soup in batches to a blender and purée until smooth. Season with salt and white pepper. Return to the saucepan and keep warm over low heat while making the garnish.

CRABMEAT GARNISH

In a glass or ceramic bowl, gently combine the crabmeat, red bell pepper, basil, olive oil, lime juice, and garlic.

To serve, mound the crab mixture into shallow soup bowls. Ladle the soup around the crab mixture. Sprinkle with the chives and serve immediately.

YIELD: 6 SERVINGS

CORN AND SQUASH SOUP

2 tablespoons butter

1 large leek, white part only, chopped

1 cup chopped sweet onion, such as Vidalia

1 teaspoon minced garlic

4 cups sweet corn (about 4 ears), husked, or 4 cups frozen organic corn, thawed

1 pound yellow summer squash, cut crosswise into ½-inch-thick pieces

1 tablespoon chopped fresh sage

Pinch chipotle powder

5 cups low-sodium store-bought chicken stock, or homemade

1 cup heavy cream

Salt and freshly ground white pepper

CRABMEAT GARNISH

12 ounces crabmeat, preferably Dungeness or blue crab, picked over for shell bits

½ cup finely diced jarred roasted red bell pepper

2 tablespoons chopped fresh basil

1½ tablespoons extra virgin olive oil

1 tablespoon fresh lime juice

½ teaspoon finely minced garlic

2 tablespoons minced chives

Tamarind's Chicken Soup with Wild Lime and Rice Stick Noodles

YIELD: 4 TO 6 SERVINGS

3 cups low-sodium store-bought chicken broth or stock, or homemade

2 (13½-ounce) cans light coconut milk, well-shaken

3 fresh lemongrass stalks, 1 or 2 outer leaves and all but the lower 6 inches discarded, finely minced

2 tablespoons peeled and coarsely chopped fresh ginger

2 tablespoons coarsely chopped, fresh or frozen, peeled *galangal*, thawed (optional)

½ serrano chile or jalapeño, deseeded, deveined, and sliced

1½ teaspoons Asian chili garlic sauce or ½ teaspoon crushed red pepper flakes

4 medium cloves garlic, peeled and lightly crushed

2 tablespoons Thai or Vietnamese fish sauce

2 wild lime leaves (also called *kaffir* lime leaves), fresh or frozen, finely sliced

½ pound dried rice vermicelli noodles (also called rice stick) or narrow dried rice noodles

¾ pound skinless, boneless chicken breast (about 1 whole breast), thinly sliced crosswise then cut lengthwise into thin strips

2 tablespoons fresh lime juice

Salt

¼ cup sliced fresh basil, preferably Thai basil (for garnish)

2 tablespoons fresh cilantro leaves (for garnish)

Here's an aromatic soup from the menu of our pan-Asian restaurant, Tamarind, onboard the *Eurodam*. If you wish, you can make the soup base up to three days in advance and add shredded rotisserie chicken instead of cooking raw chicken in the soup. For a change, substitute about three-quarters of a pound of peeled and deveined medium shrimp for the chicken.

In a large saucepan, combine the chicken broth, coconut milk, lemongrass, ginger, *galangal*, serrano chili, chili garlic sauce, garlic, fish sauce, and lime leaves. Bring to a simmer over high heat. Reduce heat to low and continue simmering, uncovered, for 15 minutes. Remove from the heat, cover the pan, and let the soup steep for 30 minutes.

Strain the soup through a sieve, discarding the solids. Return the soup to the saucepan; place the soup over medium heat and gently bring it to a simmer uncovered. The soup can also be stored in a bowl, covered, and kept in the refrigerator for up to 3 days.

Bring a large pot of salted water to a boil. Meanwhile, in a large bowl, soak the noodles in warm water and cover for 15 minutes. Drain the noodles and add them to the saucepan of boiling salted water. Cook until tender, about 1 to 2 minutes; drain immediately and rinse them under cold water; set aside.

Add the chicken to the simmering soup, and continue to simmer gently until cooked through, about 8 minutes. While the chicken is

GALANGAL AND KAFFIR LIME LEAVES

- Fresh or frozen *galangal* can be found in Chinese and Southeast Asian grocery stores. Related to ginger, it adds a pleasantly earthy pungency to many traditional Southeast Asian dishes. Galangal is much firmer than ginger and is usually strained out before serving. Dried galangal products lack the flavor of fresh or frozen.

- Wild lime leaves, also known as *kaffir* lime leaves, lend a citrusy aroma and flavor to soups and braises. They resemble two leaves joined end to end and are sold fresh or frozen in Asian markets. Dried lime leaves have little flavor and should be avoided.

If you can't find these items at specialty food stores, try online sources such as Amazon or Adriana's Caravan: www.adrianascaravan.com.

cooking, heat the noodles in the microwave in 30-second intervals to rewarm. Cut the noodles with scissors if too long and divide them among warm soup bowls.

To serve, add the lime juice to the soup and season with salt. Ladle the soup over the noodles in the soup bowls and sprinkle with the basil and cilantro. Serve with extra lime slices and Asian chili garlic sauce on the side.

Roasted Zucchini Bisque

YIELD: 4 TO 5 SERVINGS

1½ pounds zucchini, halved lengthwise and seeds removed, then roughly chopped

1 medium onion, chopped

1 to 2 tablespoons extra virgin olive oil

Salt and freshly ground black pepper

2½ cups low-sodium store-bought chicken broth or stock, or homemade

½ teaspoon nutmeg

1 teaspoon chopped fresh basil

1 cup heavy cream

1 apple, washed, cored, and half thinly sliced and half cut into matchsticks (for garnish)

1 tablespoon homemade or store-bought basil oil (for garnish, recipe follows)

5 chives (for garnish)

BASIL OIL

½ cup extra virgin olive oil

1 bunch basil leaves, picked, washed, and gently dried

½ teaspoon kosher salt

Roasting zucchini adds terrific aroma and great depth of flavor to this soup. Because the zucchini will shrink down considerably in the oven, this is a fabulous recipe if you need to consume a swelling garden harvest.

Heat the oven to 400°F. In a medium bowl, combine the zucchini and onion. Toss with the olive oil until lightly coated. Season with salt and pepper. Spread the vegetables around a baking sheet and roast for 30 minutes, or until the vegetables are browned on the edges and very soft.

Transfer the vegetables to a large saucepan. Add the broth and nutmeg and bring to a boil over medium-high heat. Reduce the heat to low and simmer, stirring occasionally, for 5 to 10 minutes. Remove from the heat and allow to cool for 10 minutes.

Transfer the soup in 2 batches to a blender and purée until smooth, adding half of the basil to each batch. (Alternatively, you can use a handheld stick blender.) Pour the puréed soup into a saucepan and season with salt and pepper. (From this point you can store the soup, covered, for up to 3 days in the refrigerator.)

Return the puréed soup to the saucepan and bring to a gentle simmer. Add the cream and season with salt and pepper. To serve, divide the soup among warm bowls and top with the apple slices and matchsticks. Serve immediately garnished with basil oil and chive strands.

BASIL OIL

In a small saucepan, heat the olive oil just until very hot. Place the basil leaves and salt in a blender. Add the olive oil to the basil and blend until smooth. Set aside to cool. YIELD: 1 CUP

ZUCCHINI AT ITS BEST

Zucchini is available year-round but it tastes best when purchased from May through August, the peak natural growing season. It can be long or rounded. For the best flavor, choose zucchini that is younger and smaller, from one to eight inches in length. Larger zucchini can be bitter tasting and have tough seeds. Store in an opened plastic bag in the vegetable drawer of your refrigerator for up to one week.

Growing up in my home in Austria, there was always a big salad bowl in the middle of the table to be shared between the ten of us kids who would fight to get the best parts. In each of the recipes in this collection, the entire salad is the best part. | Skip all the tedious chopping involved in producing a gigantic mount of salad greens and vegetables for the sake of serving "salad." Here you'll find favorite ingredients—organic tomatoes, buffalo mozzarella, seared beef, and warm salmon—at the center of each plate. These recipes bring flavor, texture, and color combinations together deliciously for stunning salads. | On Holland America Line vessels, salads of every type, and from ethnic traditions across the globe, grace menus as both appetizers and entrées. The lineup here includes the beautifully textured Salad Canaletto, from the menu of Holland America Line's exclusive Italian restaurant Canaletto, as well as Tamarind's Seared Beef Salad, a new favorite from Tamarind, Holland America Line's distinctive pan-Asian restaurant onboard the *Eurodam*. | Holland America Line's Caesar Salad is legendary—we prepare over a million servings a year. Included here is my spin on our famous Caesar: mine is a smaller, appetizer-size portion with a fantastical presentation for high-drama entertaining. | Toss the big salad spoons and family-style bowl overboard; a small plated salad is as delectably under-stated and as elegant as it gets.

CHAPTER 4

SALADS

Beet Salad with Green Beans, Hearts of Palm, and Lemon-Chive Vinaigrette

LEMON-CHIVE VINAIGRETTE

2 tablespoons fresh lemon juice (about 1 lemon)

1 teaspoon whole grain mustard

1 tablespoon finely minced shallot

½ cup extra virgin olive oil

2 teaspoons minced chives

Salt and freshly ground white pepper

SALAD

8 baby red beets or 2 medium or large red beets (or use half golden beets)

½ pound French green beans

1 (14- to 15-ounce) can or jar hearts of palm, rinsed and drained (see note)

2 cups frisée lettuce

1 medium tomato, seeded and diced

2 tablespoons minced red onion

This salad has a wonderful texture and flavor, but you can enhance the color and elegance with golden beets and French green beans (haricots verts), if you like. Golden beets will vary in size depending on the stage of the season but are always buttery-sweet. Those that are the size of large marbles are gorgeous when served whole or halved. Slender, deeply flavored French green beans cook more quickly than the more common American variety and make for a beautiful plate.

LEMON-CHIVE VINAIGRETTE

In a small glass or ceramic bowl, whisk together the lemon juice, mustard, and shallot. Slowly whisk in the olive oil. Stir in the chives. Season with salt and white pepper. Cover and refrigerate until ready to use.

SALAD

Heat the oven to 425°F. Trim the beet greens, leaving 1 inch of stems attached, and scrub the beets. Tightly wrap the beets in double layers of heavy-duty foil; make 2 separate packages if using red and golden beets, and roast on the middle rack of the oven until tender and a small knife easily pierces the flesh, 30 to 45 minutes (1 to 1½ hours, if using larger beets). Cool to warm in the foil, about 20 minutes.

When the beets are cool enough to handle, peel them, discarding stems and root ends. If using baby beets, cut the beets in half. If using larger beets, cut them lengthwise into ¼-inch-thick slices and then into sticks. While still warm, place them in a glass or ceramic bowl and gently toss them with some of the vinaigrette. (The recipe can be made up to this point 2 days ahead; cover and refrigerate until ready to use.)

Bring a large pot of salted water to a boil and prepare a bowl of ice water. Add the green beans to the boiling water and cook until crisp-tender, 3 to 4 minutes (taste one to check tenderness). Drain and transfer to the ice water to cool. Drain and pat dry.

BEETS

Beets will keep for a few weeks in your refrigerator, so there's no reason not to buy them when you see them, especially the golden or striped (Chioggia) varieties, which are harder to find. Before chilling, remove the greens and seal them in a plastic bag.

To serve, cut the hearts of palm on the bias and add them to the bowl of beets along with the green beans, frisée, tomato, and red onion. Drizzle with more vinaigrette and gently toss until evenly coated. Divide the salad among plates and serve immediately.

NOTE: Hearts of palm are the edible inner part of the stem of a certain type of palm tree. They look like smooth white stalks and have a flavor similar to artichokes.

BRIGHT VEGETABLES

The compounds that give vegetables their color get a boost in the first moments they're heated, which is why vegetables seem to "glow" briefly right when you start cooking them. But too long an exposure to heat, even from the residual heat when cooked vegetables are left to stand, can dull the color of vegetables. That's why many vegetables cooked for use in salads, such as green beans, should be plunged in ice water immediately after cooking to maintain as much of their bright color as possible.

Field Greens with Honey Sherry Vinaigrette and Herbed Goat Cheese Crostini

HONEY SHERRY VINAIGRETTE

¼ cup sherry vinegar

1 tablespoon honey

1½ teaspoons Dijon mustard

¾ cup extra virgin olive oil

1 teaspoon salt

½ teaspoon freshly ground black pepper

HERBED GOAT CHEESE CROSTINI

½ cup fresh goat cheese

2 tablespoons mixed chopped fresh herbs, including parsley, chives, dill, mint, sage, thyme, or tarragon, or a mix of a couple of herbs

Salt and freshly ground black pepper

4 (½-inch-thick) slices of baguette or country-style Italian bread (cut at a 45-degree angle)

2 tablespoons extra virgin olive oil

SALAD

8 to 12 ounces field greens, preferably organic

2 teaspoons finely chopped shallots

2 teaspoons chopped flat-leaf parsley

The goat cheese crostini adds a layer of sophistication and flavor to a salad of mixed field greens.

HONEY SHERRY VINAIGRETTE

Whisk together the vinegar, honey, and mustard in a small glass bowl. Slowly whisk in the olive oil. Season with salt and pepper. Cover and refrigerate until ready to use.

HERBED GOAT CHEESE CROSTINI

Heat the oven to 375°F. Combine the goat cheese and herbs in a small bowl. Season with salt and pepper. Reserve.

Brush the bread slices with olive oil and arrange them on a baking sheet. Bake until golden, 5 to 8 minutes. Remove the toasted bread from the oven and let cool to room temperature. Reserve.

SALAD

Combine the greens, shallots, and parsley. Gently toss the salad with just enough vinaigrette to coat the leaves. Divide the salad among serving plates. Spread the goat cheese mixture over the bread slices. Top each salad with a goat cheese crostini and serve immediately.

MIXED FRESH HERBS

When recipes call for mixed fresh herbs, look for a package or bundle that is just that—mixed fresh herbs. If you can only buy individual herbs choose two or three, or buy all of them and make a pesto or compound butter (see pages 20 and 24).

Chicken and Mango Salad
with Orange Dressing

U se a mango that is not too soft. It will add a texture contrast in this salad and will also be easier to slice.

ORANGE DRESSING

In a small bowl, mash the garlic and salt to form a paste. Stir in the mustard, orange juice, lime juice, shallot, and honey. Slowly whisk in the canola oil. Whisk in the pepper and set aside.

SALAD

Season the chicken with salt and pepper. Heat the canola oil in a large, heavy skillet over medium-low heat. Add the chicken, cover, and cook through, about 6 minutes per side. Transfer to a cutting board and let cool for 5 minutes. Cut crosswise into slices.

To serve, place the spinach leaves in a large bowl and toss with just enough orange dressing to lightly coat. Divide the spinach among serving plates. Top with the slices of chicken, mango, and avocado. Drizzle with more orange dressing and serve immediately.

DEALING WITH MANGOES

To seed and peel a mango with little waste of fruit, use a small sharp knife to cut all around the mango's length (your knife won't go very deeply because you'll be cutting all along the edge of the flat seed). Next, hold a dessert spoon in one hand and hold the mango with the narrower end toward you in the other. With the spoon upside down, slip it into the cut at the narrower end and run it flush along the seed, pushing the spoon forward and from side to side, to separate the fruit from the seed. You will eventually free one half of the mango from the seed. Set the seedless half aside, turn the other half skin-side up, and follow the same process to seed it. Discard the seed. Finally, use a peeler or knife to peel the skin from each half and then slice the fruit as directed.

YIELD: 4 SERVINGS

ORANGE DRESSING

1 teaspoon minced garlic

½ teaspoon salt

1 teaspoon Dijon mustard

⅓ cup fresh orange juice

3 tablespoons fresh lime juice

1 tablespoon minced shallot

2 teaspoons honey

½ cup canola oil

¼ teaspoon freshly ground black pepper

SALAD

1¼ pounds skinless, boneless chicken breast halves (about 3)

Salt and freshly ground black pepper

1 tablespoon canola oil

4 cups baby spinach or baby arugula

1 large mango, peeled, pitted, and cut into ½-inch-thick slices

1 large avocado, halved, peeled, pitted, and sliced

Grilled Romaine with Marinated Vegetables and Toasted Cumin Dressing

YIELD: 8 SERVINGS

MARINATED VEGETABLES

1 medium jicama (about ¾ pound), peeled and cut into sticks

1 each red and green bell peppers, cored, seeded, and cut into thin strips

1 medium carrot, peeled and cut into thin strips

½ seedless cucumber, peeled, quartered lengthwise, and sliced crosswise

Juice of 2 limes

1 medium jalapeño, deseeded, deveined, and finely chopped

2 teaspoons minced garlic

¼ cup finely chopped red onion

½ cup extra virgin olive oil

½ bunch cilantro, leaves removed from stems, rinsed, dried, and finely chopped

Salt and freshly ground black pepper

TOASTED CUMIN DRESSING

2 tablespoons fresh lemon juice (about 1 lemon)

1 large egg yolk (see sidebar)

2 medium garlic cloves, roughly chopped

1½ teaspoons whole cumin seeds, toasted until fragrant (but not burnt) in a small, dry heavy skillet

1 tablespoon Dijon mustard

¼ jalapeño, deseeded, deveined, and roughly chopped

2 cups olive oil blend or light olive oil

¼ cup white wine vinegar

Salt and freshly ground black pepper

Make this colorful, flavorful salad even more festive by using blue, red, and/or green corn tortillas—homemade or purchased—for the crispy garnish. Grilling the romaine lettuce adds just a hint of smokiness, but if grilling is not an option, it can be made with raw romaine. The vegetables need to marinate for several hours.

MARINATED VEGETABLES

Combine the jicama, bell peppers, carrot, and cucumber in a large glass or ceramic bowl.

In a smaller glass or ceramic bowl, whisk together the lime juice, jalapeño, garlic, and red onion. Slowly whisk in the olive oil. Stir in the cilantro. Season with salt and pepper.

Add just enough cilantro dressing to the vegetables to lightly coat them while gently tossing. Cover and allow them to marinate in the refrigerator for several hours, stirring occasionally.

TOASTED CUMIN DRESSING

In a food processor, combine the lemon juice, egg yolk, garlic, cumin seeds, mustard, and jalapeño. With the motor running, add the olive oil in a slow stream.

Slowly add the vinegar, stopping to taste from time to time until the desired acidity is reached (you may not need all of the vinegar). Season with salt and pepper.

CORN TORTILLA STRIPS

In a 10- or 12-inch frying pan or cast-iron skillet, heat 1 inch of vegetable oil over medium-high heat until a deep-frying thermometer registers 350°F (do not allow the oil to smoke). Line a wire rack with paper towels.

When the oil is ready, add a handful or two of the tortilla strips, being careful not to overcrowd the pan, and fry until golden, 30 to 45 seconds. With a slotted spoon, carefully transfer the strips to the prepared rack to drain. Season with salt. Repeat with the remaining tortilla strips, checking the oil temperature in between batches and adjusting the heat accordingly. (Strips can be stored at room temperature in an airtight container for up to 5 days.)

GRILLED ROMAINE

Heat a grill (charcoal, gas, or electric) to medium hot (when you can hold your hand 5 inches above the rack for 3 to 4 seconds). In a large mixing bowl, combine the romaine, olive oil, and garlic.

Grill the romaine hearts, cut-sides down, on a lightly oiled grill rack until grill marks just appear, about 2 minutes. Return the romaine to the large mixing bowl. (Alternatively, grill the romaine in a hot, lightly oiled ridged grill pan over moderately high heat.)

TO SERVE

Toss the romaine with just enough cumin dressing to coat the leaves. Divide the romaine among serving plates. Arrange the marinated vegetables around the lettuce. Top the salad with the tortilla strips and serve immediately.

USING RAW EGGS

You can eliminate the small risk of exposure to salmonella contamination in raw egg preparations by using pasteurized in-the-shell eggs or pasteurized egg yolks, available in pourable cartons. Liquid whole eggs in the carton are pasteurized but contain a blend of egg whites and egg yolks, so they generally aren't appropriate for recipes calling for yolks or whites specifically.

CORN TORTILLA STRIPS

2 to 3 cups vegetable or canola oil

4 (6- to 7-inch) store-bought corn tortillas, each halved and cut crosswise into ¼-inch strips

Salt

GRILLED ROMAINE

4 romaine hearts, cut in half length-wise while still attached to core

2 tablespoons extra virgin olive oil

2 teaspoons minced garlic

Chef Rudi's Caesar Salad Bouquet

H ere's Caesar salad taken to the next level. If you make the dressing earlier in the day, this salad will come together quickly and impressively.

BREAD RING

Heat the oven to 350°F. With a serrated steak knife, carefully remove the bread at the center of each slice to make a ring; you can reserve the crustless bread pieces for another use, such as making breadcrumbs.

In a small bowl combine the olive oil, butter, and salt. Brush the bread rings all over with the butter mixture and place on a baking sheet. Bake for 10 minutes, or until the bread rings are golden.

DRESSING

In a glass or ceramic bowl, whisk the egg yolk, mustard, vinegar, minced garlic, and anchovies until well blended. Gradually whisk in the oils. Season with salt and pepper. (The dressing can be made 1 day ahead. Cover, chill, and rewhisk before using.)

SALAD

Place 1 bread ring on each serving plate. In a large bowl, toss the romaine leaves with just enough dressing to lightly coat. Stand some romaine in the center of each ring. Spoon 2 or 3 small pools of basil pesto alongside.

Sprinkle each salad with Parmesan. Garnish with anchovies (if using) and serve immediately.

YIELD: 6 SERVINGS

BREAD RING

6 (2-inch) lengths of baguette (from 1 long loaf)

2 tablespoons extra virgin olive oil

1 tablespoon butter, melted

Pinch of salt

DRESSING

1 large egg yolk (see page 65 for information about raw eggs)

1 tablespoon Dijon mustard

1 tablespoon white or red wine vinegar

1 teaspoon minced garlic

2 oil-packed anchovy fillets, drained and very finely chopped (optional)

½ cup extra virgin olive oil

½ cup peanut oil

Salt and freshly ground black pepper

SALAD

3 romaine hearts, inner leaves only, gently washed and dried

2 tablespoons jarred basil pesto or homemade basil pesto (see page 20)

1 cup shaved Parmesan cheese

6 anchovies (for garnish)

Warm Salmon and Arugula Salad with Chickpeas and Tomatoes

YIELD: 6 SERVINGS

6 tablespoons extra virgin olive oil, divided

6 (5- to 6-ounce) salmon fillets

Salt and freshly ground black pepper

1 (15-ounce) can chickpeas, drained and rinsed

1½ cups chopped fresh tomatoes

¼ cup small black olives, such as niçoise, pitted if desired

Freshly grated orange zest from 1 orange plus 2 tablespoons fresh orange juice

Freshly grated lemon zest from 1 lemon plus 1 tablespoon fresh lemon juice

1 tablespoon drained capers in brine

6 fresh basil leaves, torn

5 to 6 ounces arugula (about 8 cups), tough stems removed

This main-dish salad is delicious warm or at room temperature. You can cut the recipe in half to serve six appetizer portions.

Heat 1 tablespoon olive oil in a large heavy skillet over medium-high heat. Season the salmon with salt and pepper. Add 3 fillets to the pan and cook until just opaque inside, about 3 minutes per side. Remove the salmon from the pan and place on a large plate. Repeat with the remaining fillets and another tablespoon of olive oil.

Wipe out the skillet with a paper towel. Heat the remaining 4 tablespoons olive oil over medium-high heat. Add the chickpeas, tomatoes, olives, zests, juices, capers, and basil. Season with salt and pepper. Cook, stirring, until heated through.

Divide the arugula among serving plates. Top with the chickpea mixture. Place a whole salmon fillet on top or, alternatively, flake salmon into pieces and place the pieces atop the chickpeas. Serve immediately.

Chopped Tomato Salad with Orange and Marjoram

YIELD: 3 SERVINGS

1 red beefsteak tomato

1 large yellow tomato, preferably heirloom

½ medium red onion, thinly sliced crosswise

Zest and juice of 1 orange

½ cup extra virgin olive oil

1 tablespoon chopped fresh marjoram

Sea salt and freshly ground black pepper

Marjoram, from the mint family, is similar to oregano but more refined in flavor. Its delicacy is a perfect match for raw tomato preparations.

To skin and seed the tomatoes, bring 1 quart of water to a boil. With a paring knife, cut out the stems from the tomatoes and make a small "X" in the opposite ends. Plunge the tomatoes in the boiling water and leave them in just until the skins are loosened, 10 to 20 seconds. With a slotted spoon, transfer the tomatoes to a bowl of cold water to cool. Slip off the skins and cut the tomatoes in half along the equator. Gently but firmly squeeze the seeds from the halves. Roughly chop the tomatoes.

In a glass or ceramic bowl, combine the tomatoes, onion, orange zest, orange juice, olive oil, and marjoram. With a rubber spatula, gently toss to combine. Right before serving, season with sea salt and pepper.

Mixed Green Salad with Fresh Pear, Blue Cheese, and Toasted Pecans

Choose the ripest pears, best-quality blue cheese, and a fresh assortment of greens to create this beautiful, flavorful salad that is sure to please. Take the extra few minutes to toast the pecans, which will intensify their nuttiness and add another layer of flavor.

BALSAMIC VINAIGRETTE

Combine the vinegar, mustard, shallot, and chives in a glass or ceramic bowl. Slowly whisk in the olive oil. Season with salt and pepper.

SALAD

Combine the mixed greens and shaved pear in a medium bowl. Gently toss with just enough balsamic vinaigrette to lightly coat. Using tongs, mound the salad on each plate. Top with slices of Stilton. Garnish with the toasted pecans and serve.

YIELD: 4 SERVINGS

BALSAMIC VINAIGRETTE

2 tablespoons balsamic vinegar

1 teaspoon whole grain Dijon mustard

1 tablespoon minced shallot

1 teaspoon minced chives

3 tablespoons extra virgin olive oil

Salt and freshly ground black pepper

SALAD

4 cups mixed greens (arugula, frisée, watercress), washed and dried

2 firm but ripe pears, cored, quartered, and thinly shaved

4 ounces Stilton or other blue cheese, sliced into 4 equal-size pieces

¼ cup pecan halves, toasted (see page 76)

Tuscan Bread Salad with Seared Tuna

Feel free to grill the tuna instead of searing it, for added flavor and rusticity. Grilled chicken or salmon also pair well with this bread salad.

SALAD

Heat the oven to 375°F. Arrange the bread cubes on a baking sheet. Bake until golden, 5 to 8 minutes. Remove them from the oven and let cool to room temperature.

In a large glass or ceramic bowl, combine the bread, tomatoes, olive oil, balsamic vinegar, onion, and chopped basil. Stir gently until just combined. Season with salt and pepper. Set aside.

TUNA

Heat a dry cast-iron or heavy skillet over medium-high heat until hot. Rub the tuna steaks with the olive oil and season them with salt and pepper. Without crowding (work in batches if necessary), place the tuna steaks in the pan and sear them on each side for less than a minute per side, or until they are crusted on the outside but still pink and raw in the middle.

Remove the tuna from the skillet and let it rest briefly until cool enough to handle. Slice the tuna into thin slices.

To serve, divide the bread salad among plates. Top with the slices of the tuna and garnish with the basil sprigs. Serve immediately.

YIELD: 4 SERVINGS

SALAD

1 loaf Italian bread (about a pound), cut into cubes

6 ripe tomatoes, chopped

½ cup extra virgin olive oil

3 tablespoons balsamic vinegar

½ red onion, thinly sliced

1 cup lightly packed basil leaves, chopped

Salt and freshly ground black pepper

TUNA

4 (1-inch-thick) tuna steaks, about 1½ pounds

2 tablespoons extra virgin olive oil

Salt and freshly ground black pepper

4 sprigs basil (for garnish)

Salad Canaletto

YIELD: 4 SERVINGS

YELLOW TOMATO DRESSING

1 very ripe yellow tomato, cored and coarsely chopped

½ tablespoon Dijon mustard

¼ cup sherry vinegar

1 cup extra virgin olive oil

Pinch cayenne pepper

Kosher salt

SALAD

2 red radishes, trimmed and sliced as thinly as possible

1 small hothouse (seedless) cucumber, cut into small dice or parisienne balls

¼ cup white balsamic vinegar or other mild white wine vinegar

1 red heirloom tomato, cored and sliced into wedges

1 yellow heirloom tomato, cored and sliced into wedges

1 ball buffalo mozzarella, cut into 8 wedges

1 small red onion, thinly sliced

12 fresh basil leaves, washed and gently dried

Sea salt and freshly ground black pepper

We serve this salad at our Italian restaurant Canaletto onboard the *Eurodam*. For even more dazzle, sprinkle the salad with the Basil Oil (see page 56).

YELLOW TOMATO DRESSING

Combine the tomato, mustard, and vinegar in a blender. Slowly add the olive oil in a steady stream with the blender running. Season with cayenne pepper and kosher salt. Set aside.

SALAD

Combine the radishes, cucumber, and vinegar in a small bowl. Allow to marinate for 2 to 3 minutes.

To serve, use a slotted spoon to remove the radishes and cucumber from the vinegar and divide among plates. Ladle the reserved tomato dressing on the plates and top with the tomato wedges, mozzarella, red onion, and basil. Season the tomatoes with sea salt and freshly ground black pepper. Serve immediately.

PARISIENNE BALLS

Parisienne balls are made with a very small melon scoop, called a parisienne scoop, which can be found in kitchenware or restaurant supply stores. The scoop creates garnishes that are easy, elegant, and even fun—children just may eat their vegetables if they look like multicolored balls.

Tamarind's Seared Beef Salad

YIELD: 4 TO 6 SERVINGS

SESAME GINGER DRESSING

½ cup unseasoned rice wine vinegar

½ cup sugar

¼ cup soy sauce

1 tablespoon chopped fresh ginger

1 tablespoon minced shallots

2 tablespoons minced garlic

2 tablespoons chopped scallions

1 tablespoon black or white sesame seeds, toasted

1 tablespoon Sriracha or *sambal oelek* chili sauce

Zest and juice of 1 lime

¼ cup peanut oil

2 tablespoons pure sesame oil

Salt and freshly ground white pepper

STEAK AND SALAD

1 (¾-pound) piece flank steak

2 tablespoons vegetable oil, divided

Salt and freshly ground white pepper

½ cup stemmed, thinly sliced shiitake mushrooms or canned whole straw mushrooms, drained

6 cups fresh baby spinach

½ cup slivered almonds, toasted

1 small leek, white and light green parts only, cleaned and thinly sliced

½ cup diced yellow bell peppers

½ hothouse (seedless) cucumber, peeled, halved lengthwise, and cut into matchsticks

1 cup thin asparagus spears, lightly steamed and quickly cooled

This signature beef salad is served at our new pan-Asian restaurant, Tamarind, onboard the *Eurodam*. Sriracha sauce gives the dressing its spicy heat. It can be found at Asian markets and in the Asian foods sections of some supermarkets.

SESAME GINGER DRESSING

In a glass or ceramic bowl, whisk together all the ingredients except for the peanut and sesame oils, salt, and white pepper. Slowly whisk in the peanut oil and then the sesame oil. Season with salt and white pepper. Cover and refrigerate until ready to use.

STEAK AND SALAD

In a glass baking dish, combine the steak and ¾ cup sesame ginger dressing. Turn the steak all over to coat. Cover and let marinate for 3 hours in the refrigerator, turning occasionally. (Bring to room temperature before cooking.)

Heat a dry 10-inch heavy skillet (preferably cast-iron) over high heat until hot. Remove the steak from the marinade and pat dry with paper towels. Season with salt and pepper. Add 1 tablespoon vegetable oil to the hot skillet and then add the steak. Cook the steak, turning once, 5 to 7 minutes total for medium rare (an internal temperature of 125°F). Transfer to a cutting board and allow to rest for 5 minutes.

Meanwhile, add the remaining 1 tablespoon vegetable oil to the skillet and sauté the mushrooms over medium heat for 1 minute. Add ¼ cup of sesame ginger dressing and continue to cook and stir for 2 minutes longer. Remove from the heat and set aside to cool slightly.

Combine the remaining ingredients in a large bowl and toss with just enough dressing to lightly coat. Divide the salad mixture among the serving plates and top with the mushrooms. Cut the steak across the grain into thin slices and arrange on the salads. Pour any accumulated juices over the meat and serve the salads immediately.

TOASTING NUTS

Toast nuts, such as almonds, in a shallow pan in a 350-degree oven for 5 to 7 minutes, stirring occasionally, until fragrant and lightly golden. Toast seeds, such as sesame seeds, in a small heavy skillet over medium heat, shaking constantly, until fragrant and just golden, 2 to 3 minutes.

Penne, spaghetti, rigatoni, linguini, orecchiette, Creole rice, risotto . . . comfort and sophistication; filling without being heavy. Well-prepared pasta and rice dishes always offer the best of both worlds—and the flavors of the entire world. | The globe-trotting travelers aboard Holland America Line cruises look for authenticity of flavor and ingenuity of presentation in every pasta and rice dish served. Naturally, they find it. Our pasta and rice dishes remain eternally high on the list of most-requested menu items. | Pasta and rice are such versatile ingredients upon which to build an exciting recipe because, essentially, each presents a blank canvas to layer with color, texture, and style. Regardless, however, of the additional ingredients, be sure to give the star its due attention and take care not to overcook the pasta or rice. | When serving, keep portion sizes modest for the most elegant presentations. People can always request a second helping, and with these Holland America Line favorites, you can be sure they will do just that.

CHAPTER 5

PASTA & RICE

Penne with Tomato, Fresh Mozzarella, Basil, and Shaved Parmigiano-Reggiano

YIELD: 4 SERVINGS

1 tablespoon salt

1 pound dried penne or other tubular pasta shape

2 cups Basic Tomato Sauce (see page 22)

2 to 3 vine-ripened tomatoes, peeled, seeded, and chopped to make about 1 cup

Freshly ground black pepper

1 large ball fresh mozzarella, cubed

2 tablespoons chopped fresh basil

2 tablespoons extra virgin olive oil

1 (2- to 4-ounce) piece Parmigiano-Reggiano cheese, shaved into curls with a cheese slicer or a vegetable peeler

Because this is a recipe with few ingredients and a simple preparation, use the best-quality ones you can buy. To cut preparation time you can chop the tomatoes without peeling or seeding them.

Bring a large pot of cold water to a boil then add 1 tablespoon salt and the penne. Return to a boil and cook, stirring occasionally, until the pasta is slightly less than al dente, 8 to 11 minutes.

While the pasta cooks, reheat 2 cups of the Basic Tomato Sauce in a saucepan and add the fresh chopped tomatoes. Cook, stirring, for 1 minute over medium heat.

Drain the pasta in a colander and return it to its cooking pot. Add the reheated tomato sauce and place over medium heat. Mix very well and sauté for 1 minute, stirring the pasta vigorously with a wooden spoon. Season with salt and pepper. Add the mozzarella and fresh chopped basil and quickly toss to combine. Divide the pasta among serving plates. Drizzle with the olive oil and top with the cheese shavings. Serve immediately.

PEELING TOMATOES

It's easy to skin the tomatoes for this recipe using the water that you're boiling for the pasta. To skin and seed tomatoes, use a paring knife to cut out the stems from the tomatoes and make a small "X" in the opposite ends. Plunge the tomatoes in the boiling water and leave them in just until the skins are loosened, 10 to 20 seconds. With a slotted spoon, transfer the tomatoes to a bowl of cold water to cool. Slip off the skins and cut the tomatoes in half along the equator. Gently but firmly squeeze the seeds from the halves. Now you're ready to chop or dice.

Linguini with Zucchini and Red Bell Pepper

YIELD: 4 TO 6 SERVINGS

1¼ cups half-and-half or light cream

Grated zest of 1 lemon

2 teaspoons minced fresh thyme, mint, or basil leaves

Salt and freshly ground white pepper

1 tablespoon salt

1 pound dried linguini

1 tablespoon extra virgin olive oil

1 tablespoon minced garlic

1 pound zucchini, cut into thin strips about 2½ to 3 inches long

3 large red and/or yellow bell peppers, cored, seeded, and cut into thin strips

2 ounces goat cheese, at room temperature

4 to 6 shavings Parmigiano-Reggiano or Pecorino Romano cheese (for garnish) plus ¾ cup freshly grated Parmigiano or Romano for serving

This light and colorful pasta gets a lift from a bit of tangy goat cheese and nuance from fresh herbs—whichever kind you may have on hand. Like many pasta dishes, this combination is adaptable. Feel free to add or substitute ingredients, such as diced tomato or halved cherry tomatoes or sliced black olives, carrots, leeks, or artichoke hearts; slivered fresh basil; minced chives; snow peas; chopped ham; smoked salmon; crumbled bacon; or sautéed goat cheese.

Bring a large pot of cold water to a boil. In a small saucepan, heat the half-and-half, lemon zest, and thyme over medium-low heat for 5 minutes, taking care that it doesn't boil. Remove from the heat and season with salt and white pepper. Cover and set aside to infuse.

Add 1 tablespoon salt and the linguini to the boiling water. Return to a boil and cook, stirring occasionally, until the pasta is tender but firm, 9 to 12 minutes.

While the pasta cooks, heat the olive oil in a 12- or 14-inch nonstick skillet over medium-high heat. Add the garlic and cook, stirring frequently, until fragrant, 15 to 30 seconds. Immediately add the zucchini and peppers and cook until tender, about 5 minutes longer. Season with salt and white pepper.

Place the half-and-half mixture back on medium-low heat and bring to a simmer. Immediately remove from the heat and whisk in the goat cheese.

As soon as the linguini is ready, reserve a coffee-cup full of cooking liquid and then drain the linguini in a colander. Return the pasta to its cooking pot, add the vegetables and half-and-half mixture, and toss to combine. Add any reserved cooking liquid if the pasta seems dry, and season with salt and white pepper. Divide the linguini among the plates, garnish with the shaved Parmigiano-Reggiano cheese, and serve immediately with the freshly grated cheese on the side.

Orecchiette with Sausage and Escarole

C hewy and savory, these "little ears" of pasta catch the bits of greens and tomato in the sauce and make for addictive eating.

Bring a large pot of cold water to a boil. In a large, deep skillet, heat the olive oil over medium-high heat. Add the sausage and cook until browned on all sides, about 8 minutes. With a slotted spoon, transfer the sausage to a cutting board. Remove the skillet from the heat and carefully pour out all but about 1 tablespoon fat.

Add 1 tablespoon salt and the orecchiette to the boiling water. Return to a boil and cook, stirring occasionally, until the pasta is tender but firm, 9 to 12 minutes.

While the pasta cooks, place the reserved sausage skillet over medium heat. Add the garlic and the escarole and cook, stirring, until the escarole is completely wilted, about 4 minutes. Add the tomatoes, oregano, and crushed red pepper and stir for 15 seconds. Add the wine and simmer for 2 minutes.

When the sausage is cool enough to handle, slice it into ¼-inch pieces and return it to the skillet. Add the broth and simmer for 2 minutes more, to allow the flavors to blend. Season with salt and pepper.

As soon as the orecchiette is ready, reserve a coffee-cup full of cooking liquid and then drain the orecchiette in a colander. Return the pasta to its cooking pot and toss with the escarole mixture. Add any reserved cooking liquid if the pasta seems dry and season with salt and pepper. To serve, divide the pasta among the plates, garnish with the shaved Pecorino Romano cheese, and serve immediately with the freshly grated Romano on the side.

YIELD: 3 TO 4 SERVINGS

1 tablespoon pure olive oil

4 links sweet Italian sausage

1 tablespoon salt

8 ounces dried orecchiette or medium-size shell pasta

1 tablespoon minced garlic

1 large head escarole (about 1 pound), outer leaves removed and remaining leaves cut crosswise into 1-inch ribbons and rinsed thoroughly (discard core)

2 vine-ripened tomatoes, peeled, seeded, and chopped (see page 80)

2 teaspoons minced fresh oregano leaves or 1 teaspoon dried oregano

Small pinch crushed red pepper (optional)

½ cup dry white wine, such as Sauvignon Blanc, or an equal amount chicken broth or stock

1 cup low-sodium store-bought chicken broth or stock, or homemade

Freshly ground black pepper

3 to 4 shavings Pecorino Romano cheese (for garnish) plus ½ cup freshly grated Romano for serving

Risotto with Asparagus and Fontina Cheese

1 (14- or 15-ounce) can low-sodium store-bought chicken broth or stock mixed with 3 cups water, or 5 cups homemade

½ pound asparagus, trimmed and cut into 2-inch lengths

3 tablespoons extra virgin olive oil

1 cup chopped onion

1 teaspoon minced garlic

1½ cups Arborio rice or California-grown medium-grain white rice

½ cup dry white wine, such as Sauvignon Blanc

2 tablespoons (¼ stick) butter or 2 tablespoons heavy cream

½ cup grated Italian fontina cheese

¼ cup freshly grated Parmigiano-Reggiano cheese plus 6 shavings Parmigiano-Reggiano cheese (for garnish)

Salt and freshly ground black pepper

⅓ cup homemade or store-bought basil oil (for garnish, see page 56)

2 vine-ripened tomatoes, peeled, seeded, and chopped (optional, see page 80, Peeling Tomatoes)

It's easy to turn this risotto into a hearty seafood dish. Sauté 1 pound shrimp with garlic in butter and olive oil and fold it in at the end along with the asparagus. (For even more shrimp flavor, simmer the broth with the shrimp shells for 20 minutes and then strain them out.) A shrimp risotto would be rich enough with the fontina cheese alone, but keep the Parmigiano-Reggiano for its terrific bite. For added flavor, you can replace the butter with Tarragon Butter (see page 24).

In a saucepan, bring the chicken broth/water mixture to a simmer over medium-low heat. Add the asparagus pieces and cook until almost tender (they will finish cooking in the risotto). With a slotted spoon, remove the asparagus and transfer to a small bowl; reserve. Keep the broth mixture at a low simmer.

In a 5- or 6-quart heavy pot, heat the olive oil over medium-low heat. Add the onion and garlic and cook, stirring, until the onion is softened and transparent but not browned, about 4 minutes.

Add the rice and stir constantly for 1 minute so the rice is thoroughly coated with the olive oil and becomes infused with it, (but does not brown). Increase the heat to medium-high and add the wine. Simmer briskly, stirring constantly, until the wine is absorbed, about 1 minute. Add 2 cups broth/water mixture and bring to a boil. Reduce the heat to medium-low and simmer, stirring occasionally, until the bottom of the pan is dry when the rice is pulled back with a spoon, 5 to 8 minutes.

Begin ladling more hot broth, about ½ cup at a time, into the rice, letting the rice simmer briskly and stirring constantly, until each addition is almost completely absorbed before adding the next one. Stop adding the broth when the rice is creamy looking but still somewhat firm (al dente) in the center, 13 to 17 minutes. (Any leftover broth can be used for thinning the risotto before serving.)

Add the reserved asparagus to the risotto and gently stir for 10 seconds to reheat. Stir in the butter, fontina, and grated Parmigiano-Reggiano. Season with salt and pepper and divide among plates. To serve, drizzle with the basil oil and sprinkle with the tomato, if using, and shaved Parmigiano-Reggiano cheese.

Rigatoni with Cauliflower, Parsley, and Hazelnuts

YIELD: 3 TO 4 SERVINGS

1 large head cauliflower or broccoflower, trimmed and cut into small florets

1 tablespoon salt

½ cup extra virgin olive oil

1½ tablespoons minced garlic

Small pinch of crushed red pepper or more to taste, depending on the spiciness of the olive oil you use

Freshly ground black pepper

8 ounces dried rigatoni, about 1 inch or so in length

½ cup chopped flat-leaf parsley

1 cup freshly grated Pecorino Romano cheese

¼ cup toasted hazelnuts, chopped

This recipe calls for less pasta because the cauliflower takes on a wonderful texture and appearance that seems to mimic the pasta itself. It makes a beautiful first course, or a terrific main course with a starter salad.

Place the cauliflower florets in a bowl of cold water to soak. Bring a large pot of cold water to a boil and add 1 tablespoon salt. Drain the cauliflower florets and add them to the boiling water, cooking until tender, about 6 minutes. With a strainer or a slotted spoon, remove the cauliflower and retain the water for cooking the pasta. Transfer the cauliflower to a bowl and set aside.

In a large skillet, heat the olive oil over medium heat. Add the garlic and crushed red pepper and stir until the garlic releases its fragrance but is still pale and not brown, about 1 minute. Add the reserved cauliflower and cook, stirring gently, over medium-low heat until it becomes infused with the garlic flavor but still remains generally intact, 10 to 12 minutes. Season with salt and pepper.

Meanwhile, bring the reserved water back to a boil and add the rigatoni. Return to a boil and cook, stirring occasionally, until the pasta is just slightly less than al dente, 8 to 11 minutes.

As soon as the rigatoni is done, reserve a coffee-cup full of cooking liquid and then drain the rigatoni in a colander. Return the pasta to its cooking pot and scrape the cauliflower mixture into it. Add the parsley and toss to combine. Cook over medium-low heat for 1 minute, tossing the pasta gently. Add any reserved cooking liquid if the pasta seems dry, and season with salt and pepper.

Toss the pasta with half of the Pecorino Romano. Sprinkle with the chopped hazelnuts and serve with the remaining cheese.

TOASTING SHELLED HAZELNUTS

To toast shelled hazelnuts, heat the oven to 350°F. Place the hazelnuts in 1 layer in a baking or pie pan and bake for 10 to 15 minutes, or until they are lightly colored (overbaking will impart a bitter taste). Wrap the nuts in a kitchen towel and let sit for 1 minute, then rub them together while still in the towel to loosen their skins. Let cool completely and discard the loose skins (don't worry if some skin remains on the hazelnuts).

Creole Rice with Sausage and Shrimp

This New Orleans–inspired combination of rice with sausage and shrimp should fill you up fine, but if you have any rotisserie chicken on hand, shred a bit and add it at the end along with the shrimp. Serve to fun-lovin' friends with salad, corn bread, and a selection of hot sauces.

In a large, heavy Dutch oven or 6- or 8-quart high-sided sauté pan about 12 inches in diameter, heat the olive oil over medium-high heat until shimmering but not smoking. Add the onions, half the scallions, celery, bell pepper, garlic, jalapeños, Creole seasoning, cayenne, thyme, and bay leaves. Cook, stirring occasionally, until the vegetables have softened, about 12 minutes. Add the rice and continue to stir until it is well coated with the olive oil and the vegetables are tender, about 3 minutes.

 Add the sausage, broth, and tomatoes, and bring to a simmer over high heat. Immediately reduce the heat to low, cover, and cook until the rice is almost tender, about 25 minutes (gently stir once after 15 minutes from the bottom up). Scatter the shrimp over the rice, replace the cover, and continue to cook until the rice is fully tender and the shrimp are opaque and cooked through, about 5 minutes. Remove the bay leaves and season with salt and cayenne. Divide among the plates and sprinkle with the remaining scallions. Serve immediately.

FASTER PREP TIPS

- You can finely chop the onion, half the scallions, celery, green bell pepper, garlic (about 6 medium cloves), and jalapeños together in the food processor. Use the pulse button so the mixture doesn't turn into a purée.

- In place of canned tomatoes and jalapeño, try using canned chopped tomatoes that include chili peppers or jalapeños.

YIELD: 10 SERVINGS

¼ cup pure olive oil

1 large or 2 medium yellow onions, chopped

7 scallions, trimmed and chopped, divided

4 medium celery stalks, diced

1 large green bell pepper, stemmed, seeded, and chopped

2 tablespoons minced garlic

1 to 2 jalapeños, deseeded, deveined, and diced

1 tablespoon Creole seasoning or more to taste

½ teaspoon cayenne pepper or more to taste, depending on the spiciness of the sausage used

1 teaspoon dried thyme

2 Turkish or 1 California bay leaf

3 cups long-grain white rice

1 pound andouille sausage (pork or chicken), chorizo, or linguiça, cut into ½-inch slices

1 (32-ounce) carton low-sodium store-bought chicken or vegetable broth

1 (16-ounce) can diced tomatoes, with liquid

1½ pounds medium shrimp, peeled (tails left on if desired)

Seafood Penne with Saffron Oil

rizzling the pasta with the Saffron Oil is optional, but it will add color and depth of flavor. If you decide to use it, make it at least twenty-four hours in advance.

Heat the olive oil in a large skillet over medium-high heat. Add the onion and garlic and cook, stirring, for 5 minutes. Stir in the wine and reduce by half. Add the cream and Pernod and bring to a simmer. Season with salt and white pepper.

Add the shrimp and scallops and return to a simmer. Cook, stirring occasionally, until almost cooked through, about 3 minutes. Stir in the chopped tomato and chopped basil and cook for 1 minute more. Adjust the seasonings. Remove the sauce from the heat and cover to keep warm.

Cook the penne in a stockpot of boiling salted water until al dente, 6 to 8 minutes. To serve, drain the pasta and return it to the pot. Add the sauce to the pasta and toss to coat. Divide among the plates and drizzle with the Saffron Oil. Garnish each plate with a whole basil leaf and serve immediately.

SAFFRON OIL

In a small jar with a lid, crush the saffron with the back of a spoon. Stir in the hot water and let sit for 10 minutes.

In a small saucepan, heat the olive and safflower oils over low heat just until hot. Pour the heated oil over the saffron in the jar. Cover the jar, shake the contents, and set aside to infuse for at least 1 day before using.

SHRIMP STOCK

The wine in this recipe can be replaced with shrimp stock. Reserve the shells from the shrimp and roast them in a small roasting pan at 400°F for about 10 minutes. Put them in a medium saucepan and cover with an inch of water. Place over medium-high heat and when little bubbles come up to the surface, reduce the heat to medium. Never let the liquid boil and do not stir. Skim off any foam and add a small amount of any herbs and vegetables—such as sliced onion, carrots, and celery—that you wish. Cook very gently for about 30 minutes, strain and then return to the saucepan. Over medium-high heat, reduce to the quantity you need for the recipe.

YIELD: 4 TO 6 SERVINGS

1½ tablespoons pure olive oil

1 medium onion, finely chopped

2 teaspoons minced garlic

⅔ cup dry white wine, such as Sauvignon Blanc or Muscadet, or shrimp stock

1 cup whipping cream

1 tablespoon Pernod (optional)

Salt and freshly ground white pepper

½ pound medium shrimp, peeled and deveined (tails left on if desired)

½ pound sea scallops, tough muscle removed from the side of each, if necessary

2 to 3 vine-ripened tomatoes, peeled, seeded, and chopped to make about 1 cup (see page 80)

¼ cup chopped fresh basil plus extra whole leaves (for garnish)

1 pound dried penne

1 to 2 tablespoons Saffron Oil for drizzling (optional, see recipe below)

SAFFRON OIL

1 large pinch saffron threads (about ½ teaspoon crushed)

1 teaspoon hot water

¼ cup extra virgin olive oil

¼ cup safflower oil

Guests aboard a Holland America Line cruise have their pick of whatever expensive food items they might wish to have, such as lobster, filet mignon, and shrimp, to name a few. Yet, each evening a high percentage of guests will instead choose a dish featuring far more humble ingredients: poultry or pork. | On Holland America Line menus each poultry or pork preparation is every bit as elegant and indulgent as the plates featuring a "status" ingredient. Yes, even our chicken dishes are ordered in abundance and with great enthusiasm. In fact, of our generous nightly poultry offerings, chicken is the hands-down favorite: a single Holland America Line vessel will serve no less than two thousand pounds of chicken during the course of a seven-day cruise. | Poultry and pork lend themselves to magnificent partnerings with fruit in myriad manifestations, whether as a delicate chutney dolloped to one side of a pork chop, mangoes wrapped within a chicken breast, or an orange glaze that gives a delicious sheen to a pork tenderloin. The fruit not only gives the meat complex and contrasting flavor, but it also allows the cook to bring in appealing color, texture variants, and structural elements to the presentation of the final dish. | Similarly, the spice combinations that work with poultry and pork are virtually endless. In these eleven poultry and pork recipes alone, you'll find excellent uses for cumin seeds, coriander seeds, Madras curry powder, fresh ginger, Tabasco sauce, cilantro, cayenne pepper, fresh and dried thyme, allspice, cinnamon, nutmeg, and, the secret flavor ingredient of my roasted chicken, sweet paprika. | You can afford to be brave and bold with your spices when cooking with poultry or pork, because you can make all of these dazzling dishes without breaking the bank.

CHAPTER 6

POULTRY & PORK

Coriander-Grilled Chicken Kebabs with Bell Peppers and Raisin Rice

CHICKEN KEBABS

1½ pounds boneless, skinless chicken breasts or thighs, cut into 1- to 1½-inch pieces

1 tablespoon whole cumin seeds, toasted (see page 128, "Finding *Sambal Oelek* and Toasting Seeds")

1 tablespoon whole coriander seeds, toasted

4 tablespoons pure olive oil, divided

1 tablespoon minced fresh garlic

Grated zest of 2 lemons

1 tablespoon minced fresh oregano or 1 teaspoon dried oregano

½ teaspoon freshly ground black pepper

1 red bell pepper, cut into squares

1 yellow or orange bell pepper, cut into squares

Salt

10 (8- or 10-inch) bamboo or metal skewers

RAISIN RICE

¼ cup pure olive oil

2½ cups chopped onions

1¼ cups low-sodium store-bought chicken broth or stock, or homemade

¼ cup dry white wine, such as Sauvignon Blanc, or ¼ cup additional chicken broth

½ cup raisins, dark or golden

2 tablespoons fresh lemon juice

Salt and freshly ground black pepper

1 cup long-grain white rice

½ cup pine nuts, toasted in a heavy dry skillet until golden

1 tablespoon chopped fresh flat-leaf parsley

These exotically spiced chicken skewers pair up deliciously with the lemony raisin rice. If you want to use both chicken breast and thigh meat, thread them on different skewers because breast meat can overcook faster than thigh meat. Serve with spinach sautéed with ginger.

CHICKEN KEBABS

Place the chicken pieces in a bowl. Toast the cumin and coriander seeds in a small, dry heavy skillet over medium heat, shaking constantly, until fragrant and light brown, about 2 minutes. Coarsely grind the toasted cumin and coriander with a mortar and pestle or a coffee grinder. Add the spices to the chicken along with 3 tablespoons olive oil, the garlic, lemon zest, oregano, and black pepper. Mix to combine and let marinate, covered, in the refrigerator for at least 30 minutes or up to 6 hours. If using bamboo skewers, soak them in warm water while the chicken marinates.

Heat a grill (charcoal, gas, or electric) or broiler to medium-high heat. In a bowl, toss the peppers with the remaining 1 tablespoon olive oil. Season with salt and pepper. Season the chicken pieces with salt and thread them onto the skewers alternating chicken pieces with the bell peppers.

Grill the kebabs on an oiled rack set 5 to 6 inches over the heat source; turn occasionally. The chicken should be cooked through; this will take 5 to 7 minutes depending on whether you've used white or dark meat. (Alternatively, the kebabs can be broiled 3 to 4 inches from the heat element.) Transfer the kebabs to a platter. Serve immediately with raisin rice.

RAISIN RICE

Heat the olive oil over medium heat in a 3-quart saucepan. Add the onions and cook, stirring, until softened and translucent, about 10 minutes. Add the broth, wine, raisins, and lemon juice. Season with salt and pepper.

Bring the mixture to a boil and pour the rice evenly into the pot without stirring. Return to a boil and then immediately reduce the heat to low. Cover and cook until the broth is absorbed and the rice is tender, about 20 minutes. Just before serving, stir in the pine nuts and parsley.

Chicken Curry with Cinnamon Basmati Rice

YIELD: 4 SERVINGS

CHICKEN CURRY

2 pounds skinless on-the-bone chicken thighs

¼ cup Madras curry powder, divided

1 potato, peeled and cubed

1 medium yellow onion, sliced

1 large carrot, peeled and cut on the diagonal into ⅔-inch pieces

2 cups sliced fresh or frozen multicolor bell peppers

3 tablespoons vegetable oil, divided

1 tablespoon minced fresh garlic

1 (1-inch) piece ginger, peeled and minced

1 (14- to 15-ounce) can low-sodium store-bought chicken broth or stock, or 1½ cups homemade

2 teaspoons red curry paste

1 (14-ounce) can unsweetened coconut milk

1 to 2 tablespoons tomato paste

1 stalk lemongrass, cut into 3-inch pieces and pounded with a mortar and pestle or with the flat side of a knife, just until a few fibers are broken

2 wild lime leaves (also called *kaffir* lime leaves), fresh or frozen, finely sliced

¼ cup dark or golden raisins

1 cinnamon stick

Salt

2 tablespoons minced fresh cilantro

The delicious coconut milk sauce of this versatile curry can support many types of vegetables, so alter the kinds or amounts to your preference. Green beans, peas, cauliflower, eggplant, sweet potato, and zucchini are just a few other possibilities. Pappadams are a tasty accompaniment.

CHICKEN CURRY

In a medium bowl, toss the chicken with half the curry powder; set aside. In another bowl, combine the potato, onion, carrot, and bell peppers. Sprinkle the vegetables with the remaining curry powder and toss until everything is coated.

In a heavy 12- or 14-inch straight-sided skillet, heat 1 tablespoon vegetable oil over medium-high heat. Add the vegetables from the bowl to the skillet. Cook until the onions are softened, 3 to 5 minutes. Transfer the vegetables back into the bowl.

Put the remaining 2 tablespoons vegetable oil into the skillet and add the chicken. Cook until the edges of the pieces are golden, 3 to 4 minutes. Add the garlic and ginger and cook, stirring, for 30 seconds longer.

TOASTED PAPPADAMS

Pappadams—wafers made of split peas or mung beans and flavored with red pepper, black pepper, or garlic—can be eaten with each course of an Indian meal. You can buy them, ready for cooking, in packages in Indian specialty markets or in the international foods section of some supermarkets. Traditionally, pappadams are deep-fried so that they become light and airy. Toasting them under the broiler works, too. Either way they're delicious as appetizers with drinks, with main-course meals (especially vegetarian), or with chutney at the end of an Indian meal. Adjust the oven rack so it's 3 inches from the broiler's heating element and preheat the broiler. When the broiler is hot, carefully place the pappadams on the rack. After they begin to expand and bubble a bit, turn them over—they will cook quickly, so keep them as pale as possible and do not allow them to burn. (Alternatively, you can cook the pappadams one by one in an electric toaster oven.) Repeat with the remaining pappadams.

Add the remaining ingredients to the skillet, except for the cilantro and the vegetables in the bowl. Bring to a simmer and cook, partially covered on low heat, stirring occasionally, for 20 minutes. Add the reserved vegetables and cook until the potatoes are tender, 15 to 20 minutes longer (add any water if the curry begins to appear too dry). Season with salt and divide among plates. Sprinkle with the cilantro and serve with the cinnamon basmati rice.

CINNAMON BASMATI RICE

In a 3-quart saucepan, bring the water, butter, cinnamon, and salt to a boil. Pour the rice evenly into the pot without stirring. Return to a boil and then immediately reduce the heat to low. Cover and cook until the water is absorbed and the rice is tender, about 20 minutes. Fluff with a fork and let stand, covered, until ready to serve.

CINNAMON BASMATI RICE

2¼ cups water

1 tablespoon butter

½ teaspoon ground cinnamon

½ teaspoon salt

1½ cups basmati rice

Mango-Stuffed Chicken Breast with Cumin and Cilantro

T his is an updated version of a mango-stuffed chicken breast I served on various ships twenty-five years ago—a timeless combination. If you need to work quickly, skip the marinade and rub the chicken with a combination of 1 teaspoon of salt and a ½ teaspoon each of ground cumin, ground coriander, and freshly ground black pepper. Pair the chicken with couscous or quinoa.

Insert a small, sharp knife into 1 side of each chicken breast, keeping the opening you make no bigger than 1½ inches long as you move the knife in an arc to create a large pocket along the length of the chicken breast (go only two-thirds or three-quarters down its length so you don't break through the surface at the thinner end). Place in a glass or enamel bowl or square, glass baking dish.

In a food processor, combine the cilantro, garlic, cumin, salt, cayenne, and lemon juice. With the motor running, gradually add the olive oil through the feed tube until the mixture is blended. Add the yogurt and quickly pulse once or twice more. (Alternatively, create the whole marinade by hand.)

Pour the yogurt mixture over the chicken and toss to coat, pushing some marinade into the "pockets" as well. Cover and chill for 1 to 6 hours, turning occasionally.

Heat a charcoal grill to medium hot (when you can hold your hand 5 inches above the rack for 3 to 4 seconds) or preheat a gas grill to high, covered, for 10 minutes and then reduce the heat to medium. Insert slices of mango into the pocket of each chicken breast and seal the openings closed with metal turkey pins or toothpicks.

Grill the chicken on a lightly oiled grill rack, turning occasionally, until just cooked through, 10 to 12 minutes total. (Alternatively, broil the chicken for 7 minutes on each side or brown the chicken skin-side first in a large pan in butter and olive oil and then bake at 400°F for 15 to 20 minutes, or until cooked through.) Remove the pins and serve. Garnish with the cilantro sprigs.

YIELD: 4 SERVINGS

4 boneless chicken breasts, skin on or off as desired

¼ cup finely minced cilantro or flat-leaf parsley

2 cloves garlic, crushed

1 tablespoon ground cumin

1 teaspoon kosher salt

¼ teaspoon cayenne pepper

Juice of 1 lemon

¼ cup pure olive oil

½ cup plain yogurt (whole milk or lowfat)

1 mango, halved, pitted, peeled, and sliced (see page 63)

4 sprigs cilantro (for garnish)

Chef Rudi's Roasted Chicken
with Herb Roasted Vegetables

YIELD: 4 SERVINGS

3 cloves garlic, crushed plus
1 teaspoon minced garlic (for
vegetables)

1 tablespoon chopped fresh thyme or
oregano, divided

1 tablespoon chopped fresh rosemary,
divided

½ teaspoon sweet paprika

¾ teaspoon freshly ground black
pepper

3 tablespoons pure olive oil, divided

1 (3½- to 4-pound) chicken, neck and
giblets discarded

Salt

2 medium onions, each cut into 8
wedges

2 medium zucchini, trimmed and cut
into ½-inch sticks

2 medium yellow squash, trimmed
and cut into ½-inch sticks

1 pound cherry tomatoes

1 cup baby carrots

1 cup water, divided

This is my favorite method to roast chicken. It's also a great way to use compound butters (see page 24). Bring 2 or 3 tablespoons of the butter to room temperature and rub it all over the chicken in place of the olive oil mixture below.

Heat the oven to 425°F. Finely chop 3 cloves garlic, 2 teaspoons thyme, and 2 teaspoons rosemary and combine in a small bowl. Add paprika, pepper, and 2 tablespoons olive oil and mix to combine. Pat the chicken dry, place it on a plate, and rub it all over, including under the skin, with the herb mixture. Let the chicken sit for 30 minutes to come to room temperature.

Season the chicken inside and out with salt and lift the wing tips up and over the back, tucking them under the chicken. Put half the onions in the cavity. Place the chicken breast-side up on a lightly oiled V-rack in a shallow flameproof roasting pan and roast, undisturbed, for 20 minutes.

Meanwhile, in a large bowl, combine the remaining onions, as well as the zucchini, yellow squash, tomatoes, and baby carrots. Toss the vegetables with 1 teaspoon minced garlic, 1 teaspoon thyme, 1 teaspoon rosemary, and 1 tablespoon olive oil. Season with salt and pepper.

After the 20 minutes of roasting, add the vegetable mixture to the roasting pan and, using two large wads of paper towels to protect your hands, turn the chicken breast-side down. Continue to roast for another 30 minutes, adding ½ cup water to the pan after 15 minutes.

ROASTING MEAT OR POULTRY

When we roast, we are basically applying dry heat all around the item so that the outside surface caramelizes and the inside is tender. To be effective, roasting requires (1) a proper cut of meat that has either a fat cap or skin on its outer layer to protect the meat and add flavor; (2) a pan that allows air to circulate around the meat or poultry and a rack or pile of chopped vegetables on which to place the item to be roasted; (3) the correct timing and various methods to gauge the doneness of the item (including an instant-read thermometer); and (4) resting time, which allows the juices that have been drawn toward the outer part of the meat to return toward the center. Resting is also when carryover cooking occurs, because meat continues to cook and rise in temperature from 10 to 15°F after it's removed from the heat source.

Turn the chicken breast-side up again and add another ½ cup water to the pan. Roast for 10 to 20 minutes longer, or until the legs move easily up and down in their sockets and an instant-read thermometer inserted in the meaty part of the thigh registers 175°F.

Tilt the chicken with tongs so that any cavity juices spill into the pan and transfer the chicken to a platter (the juices should be clear yellow). Remove the rack from the pan, carefully tilt the pan so the juices are in one corner, and spoon out and discard the fat on the surface. With a slotted spoon, remove the vegetables from the juices and place in a bowl (cover with foil to keep warm).

Place the roasting pan over high heat and scrape up any browned bits from the bottom of the pan (adding some water if necessary) as you bring the juices to a simmer. Strain into a small saucepan and reduce over medium heat, if necessary, until the juices thicken and lightly coat the back of a spoon.

To serve, add any juices from the chicken plate to the saucepan and season with salt and pepper. Carve the chicken and divide among plates. Serve with the reserved vegetables and the chicken juice.

Broiled Duck Breast with
Thyme Sauce and Roasted Pears

YIELD: 4 SERVINGS

ROASTED PEARS

4 firm but ripe Bosc pears (about 2 pounds), peeled, cored, and cut lengthwise into 8 wedges each

2 tablespoons extra virgin olive oil

Salt and freshly ground white pepper

THYME SAUCE

1½ cups organic pear nectar or pear juice (made from pear purée and apple juice or just pear juice, without any sugar added)

1 teaspoon cornstarch

2 teaspoons vegetable oil

1 medium shallot, minced

¼ cup Calvados, Grand Marnier, or cognac

2 tablespoons purchased duck or veal demi-glace or 1 extra-large vegetarian bouillon cube, crumbled

1 tablespoon balsamic vinegar

1½ teaspoons minced fresh thyme leaves or ½ teaspoon dried thyme, crumbled

Salt and freshly ground black pepper

T hanks to upgraded offerings at supermarkets, duck breasts have become more readily available. They're easy to cook and make dinner a special occasion. Here, they're served with a flavorful sauce that comes together quickly, along with pears that can be roasted up to four hours in advance. As a quicker alternative to roasting fresh pears, however, you can sauté eight canned pear halves cut-side down in 3 tablespoons of butter and 1 tablespoon of sugar until nicely browned. Serve cut-side up on the plates.

ROASTED PEARS

Heat the oven to 425°F. Toss the pears with the olive oil in a medium bowl. Spread the pears in 1 layer on a baking sheet and season with salt and white pepper. Roast for 20 to 30 minutes, gently stirring twice, until the pears are tender and beginning to brown. (The pears can be roasted 4 hours ahead and kept at room temperature.)

THYME SAUCE

Stir together the pear nectar or juice and cornstarch in a measuring cup; set aside.

In a medium saucepan, heat the vegetable oil over medium heat until hot but not smoking. Add the shallot and cook, stirring, until translucent but not beginning to brown, about 2 minutes. Add the Calvados and cook, stirring, until the liquid is reduced by half.

Add the demi-glace, balsamic vinegar, and thyme; stir until combined. Rewhisk the reserved pear nectar mixture and pour it into the saucepan. Cook, stirring, for 2 minutes, or until slightly thickened. Season with salt and pepper; reserve. (The sauce can be kept, covered, in the refrigerator for up to 2 days.)

Remove the rack of a broiler pan, then add 1 cup water to the pan and replace the rack. Preheat the broiler with the pan 5 to 6 inches from the heat.

Pat the duck breast dry and score the skin at 1-inch intervals with a sharp knife (do not cut into the meat). Season the breasts all over with salt and pepper.

Place the duck breasts skin-side down on the broiler rack and broil for 4 minutes (for Long Island duck) or 8 minutes (for Muscovy), then turn over and broil until an instant-read thermometer inserted horizontally into the center of a breast registers 130°F, 8 to 10 minutes more for medium rare. Transfer the duck breasts to a large plate, tent with foil, and let stand for 5 minutes.

To serve, reheat the sauce, adding any juices accumulated on the plate under the cooked duck breasts, and simmer until thickened just enough to lightly coat the back of a spoon, 1 to 2 minutes. Whisk the butter into the sauce. With a sharp knife held at a 45-degree angle, cut each duck breast into thin slices and divide among the plates. Serve with the sauce and pears and, if using, garnish with the thyme, cranberries, and orange zest.

See photograph of dish on page 2

DEMI-GLACE

This is a flavorful, superreduced brown sauce that's enriched with Madeira or sherry and has the consistency of thick glaze. It's time-consuming to make at home but can be found in small containers at supermarkets with extensive butcher departments or wherever specialty meats and poultry are sold.

BROILED DUCK

1 cup water

6 (7- to 8-ounce) boneless Long Island (also called Pekin) duck breast halves with skin or 3 (1 pound) boneless Muscovy duck breasts with skin

Salt and freshly ground black pepper

1 tablespoon butter

6 sprigs fresh thyme (for garnish)

¼ cup canned or home-cooked whole cranberries (for garnish)

2 teaspoons finely sliced orange zest (for garnish)

Grilled Turkey Breast with Figs and Honey Onion Compote

YIELD: 4 SERVINGS

1 medium onion, quartered

2 cloves garlic, crushed

1 medium jalapeño, deseeded, deveined, and diced

1 tablespoon apple cider vinegar or balsamic vinegar

1½ teaspoons chopped fresh thyme leaves

1 teaspoon salt

½ teaspoon freshly ground black pepper

½ teaspoon ground allspice

½ teaspoon cinnamon

¼ teaspoon freshly grated nutmeg

3 tablespoons pure olive oil

1 (1½-pound) turkey breast tenderloin

4 fresh figs, quartered (for garnish)

HONEY ONION COMPOTE

½ cup golden raisins

¼ cup warm water

2 tablespoons mild honey

¾ teaspoon ground ginger

½ teaspoon cinnamon

1 tablespoon vegetable oil

1 tablespoon butter

1¼ pounds Vidalia or red onions, halved lengthwise, then thinly sliced crosswise

2 teaspoons fresh lemon juice or balsamic vinegar

A honey onion compote is a flavorful pairing for the turkey breasts, which can be grilled or sautéed. Serve roasted or mashed sweet potatoes alongside.

In a food processor, combine all the ingredients except for the olive oil, turkey, and fresh figs. With the motor running, gradually add the olive oil through the feed tube until the marinade is blended. (Alternatively, finely chop the onion, garlic, jalapeño, and thyme by hand and combine with the vinegar, spices, and olive oil.) Place the turkey in a large resealable bag and add the marinade. Seal the bag and turn the mixture so the turkey is well coated. Refrigerate for 8 hours or overnight, turning occasionally.

Heat a charcoal grill to medium hot (when you can hold your hand 5 inches above the rack for 3 to 4 seconds) or preheat a gas grill to high, covered, for 10 minutes and then reduce the heat to medium. Remove the turkey from the marinade and grill it on a lightly oiled rack until an instant-read thermometer inserted in the center of the tenderloin registers 165°F, about 8 minutes per side. (Alternatively, sauté the turkey: Cut the marinated tenderloin crosswise into 4 equal pieces. Heat a skillet over moderately high heat with 2 tablespoons of olive oil. Sauté the tenderloin in batches until browned and just cooked, about 3 minutes per side.)

Transfer the turkey to a plate and let rest, tented with foil, for 10 minutes. To serve, slice the turkey diagonally across the grain into ¼-inch-thick slices. Serve with the honey onion compote and optional fresh figs.

HONEY ONION COMPOTE

In a small bowl, combine the raisins, water, honey, ginger, and cinnamon. Let the mixture stand, stirring occasionally, while cooking the onions.

Heat the vegetable oil and butter in a large skillet over medium heat until hot but not smoking. Add the onions and cook, stirring occasionally, until they begin to soften, about 10 minutes. With a spatula, scrape the raisin mixture into the onions and stir to combine. Stir in the lemon juice. Reduce the heat to medium-low and cook uncovered, stirring occasionally, until the onions are very tender and slightly caramelized, about 20 minutes longer. Season with more lemon juice. (The compote keeps covered in the refrigerator for up to 3 days. Reheat to warm before serving.)

Roasted Pork Loin with Mustard Sauce and Thyme

This dish is especially for mustard lovers. Serve with parsleyed orzo or steamed baby red potatoes and asparagus or green beans.

Heat the oven to 375°F and put the rack in the lower third of the oven. Cut the pork loin in half crosswise (so it will fit in the skillet as you brown it), then pat it dry and rub it with the salt, pepper, and 1 teaspoon thyme.

In a heavy 12-inch skillet, heat the olive oil over moderately high heat until hot but not smoking. Brown the pork pieces all over one at a time, 6 to 8 minutes per piece, adjusting the heat or adding more olive oil to keep from burning the browned bits that stick to the bottom of the skillet.

After browning, transfer each piece to a flameproof roasting pan and reserve the skillet without cleaning it. Place the pork in the oven and roast for 40 to 50 minutes, or until an instant-read thermometer inserted at least 2 inches into the meat registers 145 to 150°F.

Meanwhile, combine the chicken broth, mustard, Worcestershire sauce, and Tabasco in a bowl; set aside. Pour off all but 1 tablespoon fat from the browning skillet and place over medium heat. Add the shallots and cook, stirring, for 2 minutes. Add the garlic and remaining 1 teaspoon thyme. Cook, stirring, until the shallots and garlic are softened, about 1 minute.

Stir in the mustard mixture and simmer, uncovered, until the sauce is slightly thickened and lightly coats the back of a spoon, about 7 minutes. Remove from the heat and let cool slightly. Transfer the sauce to a blender and purée until smooth (or you can use a hand-held stick blender). Return the sauce to the pan, adjust the seasoning, and keep it warm at the back of the stove.

When the pork is done roasting, transfer it to a cutting board and let it stand for 10 minutes. Skim off the fat in the roasting pan and add up to ½ cup chicken broth if there are baked-on pork juices in the pan. Bring to a boil on the stove, stirring and scraping up the browned bits, until the liquid is reduced to about ¼ cup. Stir the pan juice into the mustard sauce.

To serve, remove the string from the pork and cut each piece crosswise into 4 slices. Serve the pork with the sauce and sprinkle with parsley.

YIELD: 8 SERVINGS

1 (4-pound) boneless pork loin roast, tied by the butcher

½ teaspoon salt

1½ teaspoons freshly ground black pepper

2 teaspoons dried thyme, crumbled, or herbes de Provence, divided

2 tablespoons pure olive oil

2 cups low-sodium store-bought chicken broth or stock, or homemade, plus extra for deglazing the roasting pan

¾ cup Dijon mustard

1 tablespoon Worcestershire sauce

¼ teaspoon hot pepper sauce, such as Tabasco

¾ cup minced shallots

3 tablespoons minced garlic

¼ cup chopped fresh parsley (for garnish)

Pork Chops Brined in Cider with Cherry Raisin Chutney

YIELD: 4 SERVINGS

PORK CHOPS

3 cups apple cider

1 cup water

3 tablespoons kosher salt

2 bay leaves

2 cloves garlic, crushed

1 teaspoon whole black peppercorns

2 tablespoons apple cider vinegar

4 (10- to 12-ounce) bone-in center-cut pork rib chops, about 1 inch thick

3 tablespoons pure olive oil, divided

2 teaspoons minced garlic

2 teaspoons minced fresh rosemary leaves

CHERRY RAISIN CHUTNEY

1½ cups dried tart cherries

½ cup golden raisins

1 small red onion, peeled and thinly sliced

1½ cups apple cider vinegar

1½ cups sugar

½ teaspoon salt

¼ teaspoon allspice

Here the pork chops are browned in a skillet and then finished in the oven, but there's no reason you can't fire up the grill instead. Grill them over medium-hot coals for 5 to 8 minutes per side, depending on the thickness of the chop and the desired doneness.

PORK CHOPS

In a large saucepan, combine the apple cider, water, kosher salt, bay leaves, garlic, and peppercorns. Bring to a boil, stirring to dissolve the salt. Remove from the heat and add the vinegar. Cool to room temperature and chill, covered, until cold. (The brine can be made up to 24 hours in advance and stored covered in the refrigerator.)

Place the pork in a 13-by-9-by-2-inch glass baking dish. Pour the brine over the pork, cover, and refrigerate, turning occasionally, for at least 3 hours and up to 1 day.

Heat the oven to 350°F. Remove the pork chops from the brine (discard the brine) and thoroughly pat dry. In a large heavy skillet, heat 2 tablespoons olive oil over high heat. Add the pork chops, 2 or 3 at a time, and cook until they are well-browned, 3 to 5 minutes per side.

Transfer the browned chops to a baking sheet. In a small bowl, combine the minced garlic, rosemary, and remaining 1 tablespoon olive oil and spoon the mixture on the pork chops. Place the pork in the oven and bake for about 10 minutes, or until an instant-read thermometer registers between 145 and 150°F. Serve with the cherry raisin chutney.

CHERRY RAISIN CHUTNEY

Combine all the ingredients in a stainless steel or enameled saucepan. Cook, stirring, until the sugar is dissolved and the mixture is beginning to boil. Cover, reduce the heat to low, and cook until the onion is tender and the cherries and raisins are plump, 8 to 10 minutes. Serve hot or warm. (The chutney keeps covered in the refrigerator for several days.) YIELD: ABOUT 2 CUPS

Seared Pork Tenderloin with Orange Chipotle Glaze

Pork tenderloins are simple to prepare but are lean; they will stay juicy if they are not overcooked. Keep tabs on them as they finish in the oven and remove them the instant they have firmed up. (You can also grill the tenderloin over medium-hot heat, turning frequently.) The flavorful glaze reduces fastest in a wide saucepan, but a basic two-quart saucepan will work, too. Serve with wild rice and steamed carrots, which also taste delectable with the glaze.

Heat the oven to 425°F. In a wide saucepan or large straight-sided sauté pan, combine the orange juice, honey, and soy sauce. Place over medium-high heat and boil until reduced to about ⅔ cup. Remove from the heat and add the orange zest and chipotle. Reserve.

Season the pork all over with salt and pepper. In a heavy oven-proof skillet with a heat-proof handle, heat the olive oil over moderately high heat until just beginning to smoke. Add the pork and brown, turning on all sides, for about 4 minutes total.

Transfer the skillet with the pork to the oven and roast on the middle rack for about 10 minutes, or until an instant-read thermometer inserted diagonally into the center of the tenderloin registers 140°F. Let the pork sit in the skillet at room temperature for 10 minutes (the temperature will rise to about 155°F).

To serve, cut the pork at an angle into ½-inch-thick slices. Arrange some sliced pork on each plate. Reheat the orange chipotle glaze and swirl in the butter. Drizzle the pork with the glaze and serve immediately.

YIELD: 3 TO 4 SERVINGS

2 cups fresh-squeezed orange juice or 100-percent pure squeezed store-bought

5 tablespoons honey

¼ cup soy sauce

2 tablespoons grated orange zest

2 teaspoons minced canned chipotle chiles in adobo sauce, or more to taste

1¼ pounds pork tenderloin

Salt and freshly ground black pepper

1 tablespoon pure olive oil

1 tablespoon butter

Beer Braised Smoked Sausage with Cabbage and Apples

YIELD: 4 SERVINGS

1 large head green cabbage or
4 well-packed cups shredded cabbage
and carrot coleslaw mix (without
dressing)

1 teaspoon extra virgin olive oil

1 pound smoked kielbasa (Polish
sausage), cut on the diagonal into
½-inch slices

1 medium onion, thinly sliced

1 medium tart apple, peeled, cored,
and cut into 1-inch chunks

1 tablespoon chopped fresh thyme
leaves, or 1 teaspoon dried thyme

1 cup amber beer or low-sodium
store-bought chicken broth or stock,
or homemade

¼ teaspoon freshly ground black
pepper

This is comfort food, grandma-style. Serving it in a steamed cabbage leaf freshens the look of this classic braise. If you like, place the cabbage "bowl" on a bed of mashed potatoes.

If using a head of cabbage, discard any wilted or discolored outer leaves and then pull off 4 large leaves, to use as optional decorative "bowls" for the braise; set aside. Halve the remaining head of cabbage and cut out the core. Thinly slice 4 cups of the cabbage. Wash the cabbage and thoroughly drain it. (Alternatively, use precut cabbage and carrot coleslaw.)

Heat the olive oil over medium-high heat in a large, heavy nonstick skillet until hot but not smoking. Add the sausage and brown for 4 to 5 minutes, stirring occasionally. Drain any excess fat.

Add the shredded cabbage, onion, apple, and thyme. Cook, stirring occasionally, until the cabbage is lightly browned, about 8 minutes. Add the beer and bring to a boil. Reduce the heat to low and simmer, partially covered and stirring occasionally, until the cabbage is tender, 15 to 20 minutes.

Meanwhile, bring 2 inches of water to a boil in a large saucepan with a steamer insert over high heat. Add the 4 reserved cabbage leaves and steam, covered, just until softened and bright green.

Divide the cabbage leaves among serving plates. Spoon some braised sausage and cabbage mixture into each leaf and serve immediately.

Pork Piccata

Pounding sliced pork tenderloin medallions will make an especially tender piccata with eye appeal. But you can use packaged pork cutlets instead. Their shape may not be very uniform and they may need some pounding to bring them to an even thickness, but they will taste just as delicious. Serve this lemony pork with herbed rice and green beans, sautéed mushrooms, or steamed broccoli.

Place the pork slices between heavy-duty plastic wrap. Using a rolling pin or meat mallet, gently pound them to a ¼-inch thickness. In a shallow bowl, combine the flour, salt, and pepper. Lightly coat the pork in the flour mixture, shaking off any excess.

In a large nonstick skillet, heat 2 tablespoons butter over medium-high heat. Working in batches, sauté the pork until just cooked through, about 2 minutes per side. Transfer the pork to a plate. Tent with foil to keep warm.

Using the same skillet, reduce the heat to medium and add the remaining 1 tablespoon butter. Cook the shallots, stirring, for 1 minute. Add the chicken broth and lemon juice; bring to a boil and reduce, scraping up any browned bits, for about 2 minutes. Stir in half of the parsley and all of the capers. Season with salt, pepper, and lemon juice.

Return the pork to the skillet. Cook just until the pork is lightly coated and thoroughly heated through. Sprinkle with the remaining parsley and serve.

YIELD: 4 SERVINGS

1¼ pounds pork tenderloin, trimmed and cut crosswise into 1-inch-thick slices

3 tablespoons all-purpose flour

½ teaspoon salt

⅛ teaspoon freshly ground black pepper

3 tablespoons butter, divided

¼ cup minced shallots

½ cup low-sodium store-bought chicken broth or stock, or homemade, or ¼ cup broth and ¼ cup dry white wine, such as Sauvignon Blanc, Chenin Blanc, or Pinot Blanc

1 tablespoon fresh lemon juice, plus more to taste

3 tablespoons minced fresh parsley, divided

1 tablespoon capers

On every vessel in the Holland America Line fleet, from the *Amsterdam* to the *Zuiderdam*, there is a five-star-caliber Pinnacle Grill restaurant at which filet mignon, a bone-in-rib-eye, porterhouse, NY strip, and lamb chops are ever present on the menu. The Pinnacle Grill is full to capacity all night, every night. To ensure a seat for dinner, reservations are highly recommended—upon booking the cruise itself! | Beef in one cut or another is also featured nightly on the menu in the main dining room. When the Braised Short Ribs with Garlic Cloves and Baby Carrots hits the menu rotation, it flies out of the galley. | Lamb, which is listed on the main dining room menu every other evening, is no slouch either. When a lamb presentation is offered, guests order it in droves. | The beef and lamb dishes on the Holland America Line menus are wildly popular because the meat onboard ship is of the highest quality. So whether you choose to cook the Steak Diane—a favorite from the Pinnacle Grill menu—or the delectably tender Rack of Lamb with Roasted Vegetables, it's well worth going to the extra expense of procuring the best meat you can find. | The next step is having a great, innovative recipe. Here you will find a western-style method of preparation employed with Asian flavors (Wasabi-Crusted Beef Tenderloin Steak with Teriyaki Sauce). You will also find the sensational braising/stewing technique to make the best short ribs ever, the shallow-frying technique for my favorite Wiener Schnitzel, and a stir-fry technique. | Finally, take note of the recipes for lamb with mint, rack of lamb with garlic and rosemary, and lamb with curry. Aside from providing favorite Holland America Line recipes, this chapter is like a course in meat cookery. Make every recipe and you will have learned much about mastering meats!

CHAPTER 7

BEEF & LAMB

Steak Diane

YIELD: 4 SERVINGS

4 cups (32-ounces) store-bought beef broth or stock, or homemade

1 teaspoon cornstarch

1 tablespoon water

2 tablespoons canola oil

8 (3- to 4-ounce) medallions beef tenderloin (filet mignon), about ¾ to 1 inch thick or gently pounded to that thickness

Salt and freshly ground black pepper

1 tablespoon butter

½ cup minced shallots

2 cups sliced mushrooms

¼ cup cognac or brandy

1 cup heavy cream

3 teaspoons Worcestershire sauce

1 tablespoon Dijon mustard

2 tablespoons minced parsley

For our popular Steak Diane at Pinnacle Grill, we use a wine-enriched veal stock that's been slowly reduced with vegetables for many hours. This quicker rendition is still delicious and much easier. Use a beef broth that is minimally processed (available at many natural foods supermarkets). Serve with garlic mashed potatoes and steamed carrots.

Heat the oven to 200°F. In a 3-quart saucepan or 10-inch straight-sided skillet, boil the broth over medium-high heat until reduced to 1 cup, about 30 minutes (the wider the pan the faster the liquid will reduce). Pour ¾ cup into a glass measuring cup; set aside. In a 1-quart saucepan, whisk the cornstarch with the water. Add the remaining ¼ cup reduced broth to the cornstarch mixture and cook, whisking, over medium heat until the broth is thickened and glossy. Remove from the heat and set aside.

In a 14-inch skillet, heat the canola oil over medium-high heat. Season the beef medallions with salt and pepper and add to the skillet. (If using a smaller skillet, cook in batches.) Sear the medallions for 3 minutes on the first side and 2 minutes on the other side. Transfer to a baking sheet and place in the oven to keep warm.

Add the butter to the same skillet and melt it over medium-high heat. Add the shallots and cook, stirring, for 30 seconds. Add the mushrooms and cook, stirring, until softened, about 2 minutes.

Turn off the heat and make sure there's plenty of clear airspace above the skillet. Add the cognac. While standing back from the stove, tilt the skillet slightly away from you and carefully ignite the alcohol with a long match held at the edge of the skillet. After it's ignited, move the skillet back and forth until the flames die out.

AN ELEGANT PRESENTATION

For a more elegant and refined look, as shown in the photo, you can strain the sauce before pouring it over the beef medallions. After you divide the beef among the plates, pour the sauce through a medium sieve over and around the medallions. Then spoon the mushrooms and shallots caught in the sieve on top of each medallion.

Turn the heat back on under the skillet to medium-high and add the reserved ¾ cup reduced broth. Bring to a simmer and cook, stirring, for 1 minute. Add the cream and Worcestershire sauce and bring to a boil. Cook, stirring, until the sauce is thick enough to lightly coat the back of a spoon, about 6 minutes. Stir in the mustard and season with salt and pepper.

Divide the beef medallions among serving plates. Pour any juices from the baking sheet into the sauce and stir them in. Drizzle the warm sauce partially on top of and all around the medallions. Reheat the reserved ¼ cup thickened beef broth and drizzle it over the medallions and the sauce on the plates as a contrast. Top the beef with the parsley and serve immediately.

Prosciutto-Wrapped Filet Mignon

Prosciutto wraps more easily around filet mignon than bacon slices, and it helps to protect the meat and add flavor in just the same way. If you like, substitute purchased or homemade herb-infused oil for the olive oil, herbs, and garlic (see Basil Oil page 56). Serve with your favorite flavored mashed potatoes and baby vegetables.

Heat the oven to 500°F. In a food processor, combine the basil and garlic. With the motor running, stream in ⅓ cup olive oil.

Place the steaks on a plate. Reserve 1 tablespoon of the herb and oil mixture in a small bowl and pour the remainder over the steaks and coat all surfaces. Set aside for 15 minutes.

Pat the steaks dry (it's fine if some bits of garlic and herbs remain on them). Sprinkle the steaks with salt and pepper. Wrap each filet with a piece of prosciutto just around the sides or enveloping it completely.

In a large ovenproof skillet (such as cast-iron), heat the remaining 1 tablespoon olive oil over medium-high heat. Add the steaks and cook on one side until browned, about 3 minutes. Flip the steaks and place the skillet in the oven. Cook for 3 to 4 minutes for medium rare, or to the doneness desired. Transfer the steaks to a plate and tent with foil; let rest for 5 minutes. To serve, top each steak with some of the reserved herb and oil mixture.

YIELD: 4 SERVINGS

2 to 3 tablespoons coarsely chopped fresh basil or rosemary leaves

2 medium cloves garlic, crushed

⅓ cup plus 1 tablespoon pure olive oil, divided

4 (6-ounce) filet mignon steaks (each about 1½ to 2 inches thick)

½ teaspoon freshly ground black pepper

¼ teaspoon salt

4 very thin slices prosciutto

Filet Mignon and Shrimp "Land and Sea"

YIELD: 2 SERVINGS

4 to 6 colossal or jumbo shrimp, or prawns (about ¾ pound)

½ cup pure olive oil plus 1 tablespoon extra for brushing

2 teaspoons dried oregano, crumbled

1 teaspoon freshly grated lemon zest

Salt and freshly ground black pepper

1 teaspoon minced garlic

1 tablespoon fresh lemon juice

2 (5-ounce) filet mignon steaks (each about ¾ inch thick)

This surf and turf variation—a filet mignon crowned with colossal shrimp—packs the excitement of the original but substitutes shrimp for lobster. Serve with the Quick Béarnaise Sauce (see page 23), or even more simply, top with a dollop of Tarragon Butter (see page 24).

Peel and devein the shrimp; set aside. In a glass bowl, stir together ½ cup olive oil, oregano, lemon zest, and ½ teaspoon pepper. Mash the garlic with ½ teaspoon salt and add it to the olive oil. Add the shrimp and toss to coat well. Let the shrimp marinate, covered and refrigerated, for 1 hour. Stir in the lemon juice and let the mixture stand at room temperature for 30 minutes.

Place an ovenproof skillet on an oven rack 6 inches from the broiler's heating element and preheat the broiler to high. Brush the steaks with the remaining 1 tablespoon olive oil and season with salt and pepper. Pull out the rack with the skillet and carefully place the steaks on the hot skillet (be very careful; the pan is extremely hot and any fat may spatter). Broil the steaks for 3 minutes on each side for medium rare (about a 135°F internal temperature). Transfer to plates and tent loosely with foil to keep warm.

With the broiler still on high, carefully adjust the oven rack so a broiler pan will be about 4 inches from the heating element. Remove the shrimp from the marinade, wipe them of any excess olive oil, and place them on a broiler pan. Broil the shrimp for 4 minutes on each side (be careful not to overcook).

Place 2 to 3 shrimp on each filet mignon and serve with the béarnaise sauce.

Grilled Strip Steak with Blue Cheese Butter and Spicy Pear Salsa

New York strip steak is a very flavorful top loin steak that's sometimes called Kansas City or ambassador steak. (Bone-in strip steak is commonly known as shell steak.) Here it's topped with the luscious Blue Cheese Butter; Spicy Pear Salsa is served alongside.

In a large glass baking dish, combine the olive oil, rosemary, thyme, garlic, and pepper. Add the steaks and turn to coat. Let marinate for 1 to 2 hours at room temperature or chill for up to 6 hours, turning occasionally. (Bring to room temperature before grilling.)

Preheat a grill on medium-high heat. Remove the steaks from the marinade and pat dry. Season with salt. When the fire is hot, place the steaks on a lightly oiled grill rack; cook uncovered, turning once, about 7 minutes per side for medium rare. As an alternative, cook the steaks in a grill pan or skillet.

Transfer the steaks to serving plates. Top each steak with a piece of Blue Cheese Butter. Let stand just until the butter softens, about 5 minutes. Spoon the Spicy Pear Salsa alongside and serve immediately.

CHARCOAL-GRILLING THE PERFECT STEAK

When grilling steaks, the rack should be set 5 to 6 inches over glowing coals. The coals are hot enough when you can hold your hand 5 inches above the rack for only 1 to 2 seconds. Place the steaks on the rack and turn occasionally with tongs until cooked to the desired doneness:

- For steak ½ to ¾ inch thick: rare (6 to 10 minutes), medium (10 to 14 minutes), well done (14 to 18 minutes).

- For steak 1 to 1¼ inches thick: rare (10 to 14 minutes), medium (14 to 18 minutes), well done (18 to 22 minutes).

YIELD: 4 SERVINGS

¾ cup pure olive oil

¼ cup chopped fresh rosemary

¼ cup chopped fresh thyme

1 tablespoon minced garlic

1 teaspoon freshly ground black pepper

4 (1¼-inch-thick) New York strip steaks, about 6 ounces each

Salt

4 tablespoons Blue Cheese Butter (see page 24), chilled but not frozen

2 cups Spicy Pear Salsa (see page 26)

Braised Short Ribs with Garlic Cloves and Baby Carrots

YIELD: 4 SERVINGS

1 bottle dry red wine, such as Cabernet Sauvignon or red Zinfandel

1 cup store-bought beef broth or stock, or homemade, plus extra as needed

4 pounds beef short ribs, trimmed of excess fat

Salt and freshly ground black pepper

2 to 3 tablespoons vegetable oil

2 medium onions, coarsely chopped

8 to 12 medium cloves garlic, peeled and left whole

1 (28-ounce) can plum tomatoes, drained and tomatoes cut in half

1 sprig fresh rosemary or 2 sprigs fresh thyme, or ½ teaspoon dried rosemary or thyme plus extra herb sprigs (for garnish)

1 teaspoon sugar

3 tablespoons whole grain Dijon mustard

1½ cups baby carrots

Braised short ribs are just as tender and full-flavored as beef stew, but they look much more elegant on the plate. And like beef stew, they are best made a day ahead so the flavors can integrate and the excess fat can be easily removed. Serve with glazed vegetables and polenta or mashed potatoes flavored with scallions or chives.

In a heavy saucepan or large straight-sided skillet, combine the wine and 1 cup beef broth. Bring to a boil over medium-high heat. Reduce the heat to medium and simmer vigorously until the mixture is reduced to 1 cup (the wider the pan the faster the liquid will reduce).

Meanwhile, rinse the short ribs under cold water. Pat dry with paper towels and season generously with salt and pepper.

In a large, heavy flameproof casserole or Dutch oven, heat the vegetable oil over medium-high heat. Add the short ribs in batches, without crowding, and sear for 3 to 4 minutes on every side until nicely browned. Remove the ribs from the casserole with tongs and set aside in a large bowl.

Add the chopped onions and whole garlic cloves to the casserole and cook, stirring, over medium heat until the onions and garlic are golden, about 8 minutes. Remove the garlic cloves with a slotted spoon and place in a small bowl; cover the bowl with plastic wrap and reserve in the refrigerator.

Add the reduced wine and broth, tomatoes, rosemary, and sugar to the onions in the casserole. Scrape up any browned bits from the bottom of the casserole and stir to dissolve them. Add the reserved short ribs and any of the juices in the bowl and bring to a simmer over medium-high heat. Reduce the heat to low, tightly cover the casserole, and simmer very gently for 2 hours, adding any additional beef broth at the end of the cooking time if you need to keep the juices from burning (but try not to peek for the first 1½ hours).

After 2 hours, transfer the casserole to a wire rack and cool, partially covered, until warm, about 2 hours. Use tongs to transfer the ribs to a plate and strain the braising liquid through a sieve into a medium bowl, discarding the solids left in the sieve. Refrigerate the ribs and sauce separately, covered, overnight and up to 3 days.

The next day, remove and discard the solidified fat from the sauce and put the sauce and ribs in a flameproof casserole or Dutch oven. Add the mustard and the reserved garlic cloves and bring to a simmer over medium-high heat. Reduce the heat to low, cover, and cook for 30 minutes. Stir in the baby carrots and simmer for 15 to 30 minutes longer, until the meat is almost falling off the bone and the carrots are tender.

Using tongs, transfer the ribs to serving plates. Skim off any more visible fat from the sauce and cook, stirring, until the sauce is thick enough to lightly coat the back of a spoon. Season the sauce with salt, pepper, and mustard. Pour the sauce, carrots, and garlic over the ribs and serve immediately garnished with extra herb sprigs.

See photograph of dish on page 1

BRAISING

The technique of braising involves cooking meat (often with vegetables) slowly over low heat in a relatively small amount of liquid. Braising is different from stewing in that stew meat is cut into smaller pieces and covered completely with liquid. The resulting tenderness of the meat is the same, but with a stew the sauce takes more time to reduce to the proper consistency. The best braising meats are cuts from frequently used muscles, or those attached to the bone or are moderately fatty. They include the shank, short ribs, brisket, and chuck. The muscle fibers in these cuts are held together by connective tissue that's composed primarily of collagen, a protein that breaks down into gelatin when cooked in moist heat at temperatures exceeding 140°F. Gelatin, combined with the fat in the meat, adds succulence and body to the meat, making tough cuts tender. Braising can be done on top of the stove or in the oven at a temperature of about 325°F. (Lower heat ensures the meat can cook longer to reach the required temperature for collagen breakdown without the juices burning.)

Wiener Schnitzel

YIELD: 4 SERVINGS

1½ pounds veal cutlets, cut slightly more than ¼ inch thick

¼ cup all-purpose flour

1 teaspoon salt

¼ teaspoon freshly ground black pepper

2 large eggs

1 tablespoon whole milk

2 teaspoons water

1 cup dry breadcrumbs, medium-coarse in texture, purchased or homemade in a food processor from day-old French or Italian bread

¼ cup canola oil or light olive oil, plus more if needed

¼ cup clarified butter

4 sprigs Fried Parsley Garnish, optional (see page 144)

I was born in Austria, the land of the schnitzel, so this dish is dear to my heart. Here is my favorite recipe for it. Schnitzel is an all-occasion food for Austrians, but it's eaten most commonly as a Sunday meal. It's served everywhere in Vienna from fast-food joints to elegant restaurants. You can substitute pork cutlets, or even sliced chicken breast, but veal is the most authentic and the tastiest! The traditional accompaniment, a wedge or two of lemon, balances its richness. (It's terrific with cranberry sauce, too.) If you add a few vegetables and French fries, rice, or even potato salad, you've got a meal you'll want again and again.

Heat the oven to 180°F. Place each veal cutlet between pieces of plastic wrap and pound to a ¼-inch thickness with a meat mallet. Set aside.

Mix the flour, salt, and pepper in a shallow dish. Beat the eggs with the milk and water in another shallow dish. Put the breadcrumbs on a plate, and place a wire rack over a sheet pan.

Lightly coat each veal cutlet in the flour mixture, then dip it in the beaten eggs. Place it on the plate with the breadcrumbs and pat the crumbs on both sides so they adhere and the cutlet is completely coated; repeat with the remaining cutlets.

In a 10- or 12-inch frying pan or cast-iron skillet, heat the canola oil and clarified butter over medium-high heat. There should be ½ inch

CLARIFYING BUTTER

Clarified butter is easy to make and is a good pan-frying medium because its milk solids have been separated out; this keeps the fat from burning at higher temperatures. It adds a buttery, rich flavor. In a 1-quart saucepan over low heat, bring 1 stick of butter, cut into pieces, to a slow boil until it melts and the milk solids separate from the fat, 10 to 15 minutes. When the popping and bubbling almost stop, remove the pan from the heat and let it stand for a few minutes. Use a spoon to skim the foam off the top. Slowly pour the clear yellow liquid (the clarified butter) through a small strainer into a measuring cup; discard the milk solids at the bottom of the pan. Let cool, then cover and refrigerate for up to a month.

of fat in the pan, so add more oil if necessary. When the oil mixture
is very hot, but not smoking, add just enough breaded cutlets to fit
comfortably in the pan. Cook, turning once, until golden brown, 2 to 3
minutes on each side. Transfer each finished batch to the rack and
keep warm in the oven until ready to serve.

Wasabi-Crusted Beef Tenderloin Steak with Teriyaki Sauce

WASABI-CRUSTED STEAK

1½ tablespoons wasabi (Japanese horseradish) powder or 2 tablespoons wasabi paste

1 tablespoon water

4 tablespoons (½ stick) butter, at room temperature

½ cup thinly sliced scallions

1 teaspoon minced garlic

2 teaspoons whole grain mustard

1 teaspoon sugar

1 large egg yolk

2 teaspoons prepared horseradish

¼ cup Japanese-style "panko" breadcrumbs (available in the Asian section of most supermarkets) or fresh breadcrumbs made from day-old crustless French bread

1 tablespoon peanut or vegetable oil

4 (6- to 8-ounce) filet mignon steaks (each about 1 inch thick)

Salt and freshly ground black pepper

TERIYAKI SAUCE

1 teaspoon minced garlic

3 tablespoons bottled teriyaki sauce

3 tablespoons sake, mirin (sweet Japanese rice wine), or medium dry sherry

3 tablespoons store-bought beef stock, or homemade

 erve with jasmine rice studded with black sesame seeds and a stir-fry of bok choy and shiitake mushrooms.

Combine the wasabi powder with 1 tablespoon water in a medium bowl stirring with a fork to form a paste (or just place the 2 tablespoons wasabi paste in the bowl). Add the butter, scallions, garlic, mustard, sugar, egg yolk, prepared horseradish, and breadcrumbs. Stir with a rubber spatula until all ingredients are well mixed. Set aside.

Preheat the broiler. In a large heavy skillet, heat the peanut oil over medium-high heat. Season the steaks with salt and pepper. Add the steaks to the skillet and cook until browned on both sides and cooked to desired doneness, about 5 minutes per side for medium rare.

Transfer the steaks to a rimmed baking sheet; reserve the skillet. Press equal amounts of the breadcrumb mixture onto the tops of the steaks. Broil the steaks until the topping browns, about 2 minutes. Transfer the steaks to plates.

TERIYAKI SAUCE

While the steaks rest, place the steak skillet back on the heat and add the garlic, teriyaki sauce, sake, and stock. Bring to a boil over medium heat, scraping up any browned bits from the bottom of the skillet and stirring to dissolve them. When the sauce lightly coats the back of a spoon, remove from the heat. Serve the teriyaki sauce on the side.

A TENDER CUT OF MEAT

Beef tenderloin steaks, cut from the tenderloin, are the most tender steaks you can buy. They have less flavor, however, than other cuts, so they're often enhanced with bold ingredients such as peppercorns, blue cheese, red wine reductions, or horseradish. They should not be marinated or cooked beyond medium rare. American butchers usually call all tenderloin steaks filet mignons, but the French save the term just for the cuts at the small end of the tenderloin, which are the most prized.

Spicy Stir-Fried Sesame Beef

YIELD: 6 SERVINGS

2 pounds beef tenderloin tips, sliced across the grain into ⅛-inch-thick slices

¼ cup plus 3 tablespoons soy sauce, divided

2 tablespoons minced garlic, divided

2 tablespoons finely chopped peeled fresh ginger, divided

½ cup low-sodium store-bought chicken stock, or homemade

⅓ cup hoisin sauce

1 tablespoon sugar

1 tablespoon *sambal oelek* or to taste

1 tablespoon cornstarch

¼ cup peanut or vegetable oil, divided

½ pound (about 2 medium) red bell peppers, cored and sliced into ¼-inch-thick strips

½ pound onions, halved and sliced (about 2 cups)

½ pound snow peas, trimmed

2 tablespoons chili oil (optional)

1 tablespoon Asian sesame oil

2 tablespoons white or black sesame seeds, toasted (for garnish)

4 scallions, white and light green parts only, thinly sliced (for garnish)

 his stir-fry can be as spicy as you like—just alter the quantity of chili oil used. Serve with rice.

In a glass bowl, combine the sliced beef, ¼ cup soy sauce, 1 tablespoon garlic, and 1 tablespoon ginger. Cover with plastic wrap and let the beef marinate in the refrigerator for at least 10 minutes and up to 1 hour, stirring once.

Meanwhile, in another glass bowl or a measuring cup, whisk the chicken stock, hoisin sauce, remaining 3 tablespoons soy sauce, sugar, *sambal oelek*, and cornstarch; set aside.

Drain the beef, pat it dry, and discard any remaining marinade. Heat a wok or a 12- or 14-inch skillet over high heat until a bead of water dropped on the cooking surface evaporates immediately. Add 2 teaspoons peanut oil, swirling the wok or skillet to coat it evenly. Add a quarter of the beef slices, breaking up the clumps, and cook, without stirring, for 1 minute. Stir the beef and cook until it's browned around the edges, about 30 seconds longer. Transfer the beef to a bowl and repeat in 3 more batches; use all but 1 tablespoon of the oil.

Add the remaining peanut oil to the now-empty wok or skillet and heat until hot but not smoking. Add the remaining 1 tablespoon garlic and 1 tablespoon ginger and cook, stirring, for about 5 seconds. Add the bell peppers and onions and stir-fry for 2 minutes. Add the snow peas and stir-fry until crisp-tender, 1 to 2 minutes.

Return the beef and any of its juices to the wok or skillet and toss to combine. Rewhisk the reserved chicken broth mixture and then add it to the skillet. Cook, stirring constantly, until the sauce is thickened and evenly distributed, about 30 seconds.

Transfer to a serving platter. Drizzle with the chili oil, if using, and sesame oil, and sprinkle with the sesame seeds and scallions.

FINDING *SAMBAL OELEK* & TOASTING SEEDS

- *Sambal oelek* is a Southeast Asian chili sauce that can be found in Chinese and Southeast Asian grocery stores.
- Toast seeds in a small heavy skillet over medium heat, shaking constantly, until fragrant and just golden, 2 to 3 minutes.

Quick Curried Lamb Shoulder Chops

A s an alternative to lamb shoulder chops, you can substitute 2 pounds of boneless leg of lamb, trimmed and cut into ¾-inch cubes. Serve this curry with plain basmati rice.

Grind the chile peppers to a paste with a mortar and pestle, or in a blender. Add the coriander, cardamom seeds, fennel, turmeric, basil, thyme, and garlic. Grind until smooth. (Alternatively, crush the whole spices in a coffee grinder, then add them to the chile pepper paste and continue to grind them with the turmeric, herbs, and garlic.) Set aside.

In a large heavy or cast-iron skillet, heat half the olive oil over high heat. Add half the lamb and onion and cook, stirring, until the lamb is browned, about 2 minutes. Season with salt. With a slotted spoon, transfer the lamb and onions to a bowl and repeat the process with the remaining lamb, onions, and olive oil.

Pour off all but 2 tablespoons olive oil from the now empty skillet. Add the reserved chile pepper mixture and place over medium-high heat. Cook, stirring constantly, until the mixture begins to stick to the skillet. Immediately add the broth and bring to a simmer, scraping up any browned bits from the bottom of the skillet.

Add back the lamb and onions and return to a simmer over medium-high heat. Reduce the heat to low and partially cover. Simmer, stirring occasionally, until the lamb is tender, 30 to 40 minutes.

YIELD: 6 TO 8 SERVINGS

3 serrano chile peppers, seeded, or cayenne pepper

1 tablespoon coriander seeds

1 tablespoon cardamom pods, seeds removed and pods discarded

½ tablespoon fennel seeds

1 teaspoon ground turmeric

1 tablespoon chopped fresh basil or 1½ teaspoons dried basil

½ teaspoon fresh thyme leaves or ¼ teaspoon dried thyme

4 cloves garlic, crushed

3 tablespoons pure olive oil, divided

6 to 8 lamb shoulder chops, trimmed

1 medium onion, finely sliced

Salt

1 cup low-sodium store-bought chicken or beef broth or stock, or homemade

WHOLE SPICES

If you find yourself hesitating to buy the whole spices for this recipe, remember they easily keep a year without deterioration, unlike ground spices, which begin to fade in flavor within three to six months. Coriander is found in a wide range of recipes, and freshly ground cardamom adds an exotic flavor and scent to many baked goods. Fennel seed is essential for pizza sauce.

Tamarind's Vietnamese-Style Lamb with Mint

I f you have leftover roasted or grilled leg of lamb you can use it instead with successful results. Just toss the sliced lamb with the marinade and add it to the skillet with the spinach.

To make the lamb easier to slice, wrap it in plastic wrap and freeze until firm, no more than 30 minutes. Cut the lamb into ⅛-inch-thick slices about 2 inches long.

Combine the sliced lamb, 1 tablespoon mint, soy sauce, garlic, and ginger in a glass bowl. Cover with plastic wrap and let it marinate in the refrigerator for at least 10 minutes and up to 1 hour, stirring once.

Meanwhile, in another glass bowl or a measuring cup, whisk the chicken broth, teriyaki sauce, Sriracha, crushed red pepper, and cornstarch; set aside.

Drain the lamb, patting it dry, and discard the marinade. Heat a wok or a 12- or 14-inch skillet over high heat until a bead of water dropped on the cooking surface evaporates immediately. Add 2 teaspoons canola oil, swirling the wok to coat it evenly. Add half of the lamb slices, breaking up the clumps, and cook, without stirring, for 1 minute. Stir the lamb and cook it for about 30 seconds longer. Transfer the lamb to a bowl and repeat the process with the remaining lamb and another 2 teaspoons canola oil.

Add the remaining 2 teaspoons canola oil to the now-empty skillet and heat until just smoking. Add the onion and ⅓ cup scallions and cook, stirring, for about 30 seconds. Add the spinach, snow peas, sugar, and fish sauce and stir-fry for 10 seconds.

Return the lamb and any of its juices to the skillet and toss to combine. Rewhisk the reserved chicken broth mixture and then add it to the skillet along with the remaining 3 tablespoons chopped mint. Cook, stirring constantly, until the sauce is thickened and evenly distributed, about 30 seconds.

Transfer the contents of the skillet to a serving platter. Drizzle with the sesame oil and sprinkle with the remaining 1 tablespoon sliced scallions. Serve immediately.

YIELD: 2 TO 3 SERVINGS

1¼ pounds boneless leg of lamb, trimmed

¼ cup coarsely chopped fresh mint leaves, divided

1 tablespoon soy sauce

2 teaspoons minced garlic

2 teaspoons finely chopped peeled fresh ginger

½ cup low-sodium store-bought chicken broth or stock, or homemade

1 tablespoon teriyaki sauce

1 tablespoon Sriracha sauce

½ teaspoon crushed red pepper

2 teaspoons cornstarch

2 tablespoons canola oil, divided

⅓ cup sliced red onion

⅓ cup thinly sliced scallions plus 1 tablespoon extra for sprinkling

8 ounces baby spinach leaves

½ cup snow peas, trimmed

Small pinch of sugar

1 tablespoon Asian fish sauce, such as Vietnamese nuoc mam

1 tablespoon Asian sesame oil

Rack of Lamb with Roasted Vegetables

YIELD: 2 TO 3 SERVINGS

1 whole head garlic, in one piece, excess papery husks removed, plus 2 teaspoons minced garlic

3 tablespoons extra virgin olive oil, divided, plus extra

Salt and freshly ground black pepper

1 medium red onion, cut into 1-inch pieces

1 medium yellow squash, cut into 1-inch pieces

1 cup green beans, trimmed

1 cup cherry tomatoes

1 frenched rack of lamb (7 or 8 ribs)

2 tablespoons vegetable oil

1 tablespoon minced fresh rosemary

¼ cup balsamic vinegar, reduced to 2 tablespoons in a small saucepan over low heat (for garnish)

2 teaspoons homemade (see page 56) or store-bought basil oil (for garnish)

A weeknight meal of rack of lamb may seem like reaching for the stars, but you can make it happen with this method. The vegetables can partially roast while you brown the lamb rack on the stove, and then come out when the lamb goes in. The vegetables finish roasting while the lamb rests. Roasted garlic mashed potatoes make a fine accompaniment.

Heat the oven to 425°F. Slice the tip off the garlic head to expose the cloves. Rub with a little olive oil and season with salt and pepper. Place on two squares of heavy-duty aluminum foil and sprinkle with a bit of water. Pinch the edges of the foil together to make a packet and place in the oven while it's preheating. The garlic will continue to roast along with the lamb and vegetables, and will need to be checked periodically so it doesn't burn.

Combine the onion, yellow squash, green beans, and cherry tomatoes in a large bowl. Season with salt and pepper and toss with 2 tablespoons olive oil. Spread the vegetables on a large, lightly oiled rimmed baking sheet. Transfer the garlic packet to the vegetable pan. Roast in the oven for 15 minutes; turn the vegetables once.

Meanwhile, use a boning knife to remove any scraps of meat or fat still left on the rib bones. To make the rack look its best, remove the outer layer of fat, the small bit of meat underneath that layer, and the fat underneath the meat you just removed. Slide the boning knife between the flesh and silver skin to remove that membrane.

In a heavy skillet, heat the vegetable oil over high heat. Season the rack of lamb with salt and pepper. Add the rack meat-side down with the ribs facing outward. Sear until well browned, about 4 minutes. Stand the rack up in the skillet to brown the bottom side, about 2 minutes more.

Use tongs to transfer the lamb to a rimmed baking sheet. In a small bowl, combine the minced garlic, rosemary, and remaining 1 tablespoon olive oil and spoon this over the lamb rack. Remove the pan of vegetables from the oven (whether or not 15 minutes has elapsed) and place the lamb in the oven. If the garlic head is not yet soft, return it to the oven with the lamb. Roast the lamb for 12 to 15 minutes, turning once, or until the meat is medium-rare and an instant-read thermometer inserted into the center of the rack registers around 135°F. Remove from the oven, tent with aluminum foil, and let rest for 5 to 10 minutes.

While the lamb rests, reduce the oven temperature to 375°F and return the vegetables to the oven to finish cooking (check the garlic for doneness). Continue to roast the vegetables until they are softened and nicely caramelized, up to 10 minutes longer.

Remove the vegetables from the oven and put them in a bowl. Carefully unwrap the garlic package, set aside 4 roasted cloves, and squeeze the remaining cloves into the vegetables; toss gently to combine. Season with salt and pepper.

To serve, slice the lamb between every other bone and place on the plates with the vegetables. Scatter the reserved garlic cloves on the plate and drizzle with some of the optional reduced balsamic vinegar and basil oil.

The oceans of the world are a treasure trove of exquisite flavors. Today's home cooks have a wide variety of the ocean's harvest readily available to them, from large, chunky game fish to the delicately textured flavors of sole. | On any given night, one-third of the entire menu offering aboard any Holland America Line ship is devoted entirely to seafood; our guests appreciate the diversity of selection and the care that goes into each seafood preparation. | Our chefs love to work with fish because it's so versatile and it enables them to show off their skills and creativity. Armed with the finely detailed recipes here, you too can enjoy cooking seafood with supreme confidence and flair. | Here you'll find various cooking methods for fish, such as pan frying, baking in parchment, grilling, broiling, and one technique I developed recently for poaching fish in olive oil—which gives halibut and other fish like wild Alaskan salmon succulently rich flavor and silken texture. When asked to identify his favorite recipe in this cookbook, Holland America Line Corporate Chef John Mulvaney picked without hesitation the Halibut Poached in Olive Oil on a Bed of Leeks (clearly another must-try recipe!). | Another component in creating sensational seafood dishes lies in using well-conceived marinades, rubs, and sauces. In this collection of seafood recipes, the spices and sauces import flavors from Latin, Mediterranean, or Asian cuisine to impart high flavor and color for bold results. | Let the recipe headnotes in this chapter be your comfort and your guide. They offer instruction on the various fine points of seafood cookery that we use in the kitchens of Holland America Line ships, put forth fantastic ideas for substituting different fish or ingredients, as well as provide shortcut techniques and tasteful tips for entertaining with seafood.

S E A F O O D

Grilled Red Snapper with Olives, Onions, and Peppers

This is a lighter variation of fish prepared "Veracruz style," which typically involves mixing New World tomatoes and chiles with such European ingredients as capers, olives, and herbs. Substitute any other firm, meaty fish, such as striped bass or pompano, and serve with plain rice or steamed new potatoes.

MARINADE

Place snapper fillets in a large glass dish. Season with salt and pepper. In a small bowl, combine the olive oil, lime juice, and oregano. Rub the olive oil mixture into the fillets and cover the dish with plastic wrap. Cover and let marinate in the refrigerator for 2 hours.

FISH AND SAUCE

Heat a grill (charcoal, gas, or electric) to medium-high heat. (Alternatively, you can cook the fish in a large, hot grill pan over moderately high heat or under a preheated broiler until opaque in the center, about 4 minutes per side.) In a 12-inch skillet, heat the olive oil over medium-high heat. Add the onions and garlic and cook, stirring, until the onions are translucent but not browned, about 5 minutes. Add the wine, oregano, and marjoram. Cook, stirring, until the liquid is reduced by three-quarters.

Add the bell pepper, tomato, chopped parsley, capers, and olives. Cook, stirring often, for another 5 to 8 minutes, until the sauce is amalgamated. Season with salt and pepper.

Remove the fish from the marinade and pat it dry with paper towels. Grill the fish on an oiled rack until just cooked through, about 4 minutes per side. Transfer the fish to serving plates. Top with some of the sauce, drizzle the plates with the balsamic reduction, and serve.

YIELD: 6 SERVINGS

MARINADE

6 (7-ounce) red snapper fillets

Salt and freshly ground black pepper

6 tablespoons extra virgin olive oil

3 tablespoons fresh lime juice

½ teaspoon dried oregano

FISH AND SAUCE

⅓ cup extra virgin olive oil

2 medium red onions, coarsely chopped

1½ tablespoons minced garlic

1 cup dry white wine

2 teaspoons dried oregano

½ teaspoon dried marjoram or dried thyme

1 medium red bell pepper, cored, seeded, and cut into thin strips

1 medium ripe tomato, cored, seeded, and cut into thin strips

½ cup chopped fresh flat-leaf parsley

1 tablespoon drained and rinsed capers

½ cup green olives, halved

Salt and freshly ground black pepper

¼ cup balsamic vinegar, reduced to 2 tablespoons in a small saucepan over low heat

Halibut Poached in Olive Oil on a Bed of Leeks

YIELD: 4 SERVINGS

LEEKS

2 tablespoons butter

1 tablespoon pure olive oil

4 medium leeks (white and light green parts only), split lengthwise, rinsed, and cut crosswise into ½-inch slices

Sea salt and freshly ground white pepper

HALIBUT

4 (6-ounce) pieces halibut

Salt and freshly ground black pepper

1½ cups pure olive oil

4 sprigs dill (for garnish)

Fish poached slowly in olive oil becomes silky textured and richer tasting, and retains its succulent moistness. Substitute wild Alaskan salmon or sablefish, if you like. Serve with your favorite potatoes or sliced cucumbers marinated in equal parts of rice vinegar and water with sugar, sliced scallions, dill, salt, and pepper.

LEEKS

Heat the butter and olive oil in a large nonstick skillet over medium heat. Add the leeks and stir to coat. Cook, stirring gently, until the leeks are softened and bright green, about 5 minutes. Season with sea salt and white pepper; remove from the heat and set aside.

HALIBUT

Season the halibut with salt and pepper. Line a wire rack with 2 or 3 sheets of paper towels.

In a high-sided heavy skillet that can accommodate all the fish in a single layer, heat the olive oil over medium-low heat until a deep-frying thermometer registers 150 to 200°F (the oil will be shimmering).

When the olive oil is at the correct temperature, use a slotted spatula to gently lower the fish pieces into the skillet. Return the olive oil to 150°F by raising the temperature if necessary, but lower it immediately back to medium-low or lower so that the temperature is at least 150°F but never exceeds 200°F. Then poach the fish until

POACHING LIQUIDS

Different liquid mediums are used for poaching different types of food. Meat, poultry, and fish are often poached in broths, while fruits are often poached in sugar syrups. Herbs, vegetables, and sometimes even wine can be added to the poaching liquid. Poaching in olive oil or butter imparts a luxurious texture to fish, seafood, and poultry. No matter the medium, a slow, gentle approach is key. For the moistest, most tender results, liquids should be below a boil with the surface just beginning to show some quivering movement; olive oil or butter poaching liquids should be at just the shimmer stage (150 to 200°F).

almost cooked through, 7 to 9 minutes (if the fish pieces aren't submerged in the olive oil, turn them over after 4 minutes).

With a slotted spatula, gently transfer the cooked fish from the poaching olive oil to the paper towels to drain. Reheat the sliced leeks, adding a little water if necessary, and divide them among serving plates. Top with the poached halibut and dill sprigs and serve immediately.

Grilled Salmon with
Ginger-Cilantro Pesto on Sautéed Greens

Swap out this pesto for another, if you like, perhaps an option from Chapter 1 (just omit any cheese in the pesto recipe). Serve with white or basmati rice and lemon wedges.

To make the pesto, combine the cilantro, ⅓ cup scallions, macadamia nuts, ginger, and cayenne in a food processor. Blend until the nuts are finely chopped. While processing, slowly add 6 tablespoons vegetable oil until the mixture is well blended. Season with salt and pepper. (The pesto can be made 1 day ahead. Cover; chill. Bring to room temperature before using.)

Heat a grill (charcoal, gas, or electric) to medium-high heat. Brush the salmon with the remaining 1 tablespoon vegetable oil and season with salt and pepper. Grill the salmon on an oiled rack until just cooked through, 4 to 5 minutes per side. (Alternatively, you can cook the fish in a large, hot grill pan over moderately high heat or under a preheated broiler until opaque in the center, about 4 minutes per side.)

Meanwhile, in a large skillet sauté the garlic in the olive oil over moderately high heat for 30 seconds, or until it is fragrant. Add the arugula and stir the mixture until it is well combined. Cook, covered, for 2 to 3 minutes, or until the greens are just wilted. Season with salt and pepper.

Put the sautéed greens in the center of serving plates. Top with the salmon, pesto, and sliced scallion and serve immediately.

YIELD: 4 SERVINGS

1 cup chopped fresh cilantro

⅓ cup chopped scallions, white and light green parts only, plus 1 extra scallion thinly sliced (for garnish)

⅓ cup salted roasted macadamia nuts, roughly chopped

¼ cup chopped peeled fresh ginger

¼ teaspoon cayenne pepper

7 tablespoons vegetable oil, divided

Salt and freshly ground black pepper

4 (6-ounce) salmon steaks or fillets, 1 inch thick

1½ teaspoons minced garlic

2 tablespoons extra virgin olive oil

2 bunches arugula or 3 bunches watercress, coarse stems discarded and the greens rinsed but not spun dry

Grilled Mahi-Mahi with Tapenade

YIELD: 4 SERVINGS

4 tablespoons prepared black olive tapenade (olive paste)

1 teaspoon minced garlic

1 tablespoon chopped fresh flat-leaf parsley

Juice of ½ lemon, approximately

1½ pounds mahi-mahi, red snapper, or sea bass, cut into 4 pieces

2 tablespoons extra virgin olive oil

Salt and freshly ground black pepper

Any firm-fleshed fish fillets, about one inch thick, will work with this recipe. You can substitute jarred sun-dried tomato bruschetta topping for the prepared black olive tapenade. Serve with grilled asparagus and sliced boiled new potatoes tossed with slices of roasted red bell pepper and fennel.

In a small bowl, combine the tapenade, garlic, and parsley. Stir in the lemon juice, ½ teaspoon at a time, until the desired flavor is reached.

Heat a grill (charcoal, gas, or electric) to medium-high heat. (Alternatively, you can cook the fish in a large, hot grill pan over moderately high heat or under a preheated broiler until opaque in the center, about 4 minutes per side.) Brush the fish with the olive oil and season with salt and pepper. Grill the fish on an oiled rack until just opaque in the center, about 4 minutes per side.

Transfer the fish to serving plates and top with a spoonful of the tapenade mixture. Serve immediately.

Butter-Basted Sole with Leeks

YIELD: 4 SERVINGS

4 baby leeks, tops and root ends trimmed

2 tablespoons pure olive oil, divided

Salt and freshly ground black pepper

4 (4- to 5-ounce) sole fillets

1½ tablespoons Chive and Mixed Herb Butter, softened (see page 25)

¼ cup balsamic vinegar, reduced to 2 tablespoons in a small saucepan over low heat

In this recipe, the sole and leeks can be grilled or broiled. If grilling, use a hinged wire grill basket so the fish doesn't fall apart. If you like, substitute flounder, halibut, or cod.

Heat a grill (charcoal, gas, or electric) to medium-high heat. (Alternatively, you can broil the leeks under a preheated broiler.) Split the leeks lengthwise, rinse out any dirt, and pat them dry. Brush the leeks with 1 tablespoon olive oil and season with salt and pepper. Grill or broil until softened and well marked, 6 to 8 minutes.

Meanwhile, brush the fish with 1 tablespoon olive oil and season with salt and pepper. Place in an oiled grill basket and grill until just opaque in the center, about 4 minutes total, or broil for about 4 minutes.

Transfer the fish and leeks to serving plates. Top with the herb butter; serve with reduced balsamic vinegar.

Stir-Fried Shrimp with Snow Peas

Like most stir-fries, this one comes together in just a few minutes once you've prepared the ingredients. Serve with cooked white or brown rice.

In a small bowl, whisk the clam juice, mirin, oyster sauce, soy sauce, and cornstarch; set aside.

In a large nonstick frying pan, heat the peanut oil over medium-high heat. Add the shrimp and cabbage and cook, stirring, for 2 minutes. Stir in the snow peas, ginger, and garlic. When the garlic becomes fragrant (about 30 seconds), add the sherry and reduce for 2 minutes.

Rewhisk the clam juice mixture and add it to the shrimp and cabbage. Cook, stirring, until thickened. Season with salt and pepper. Remove from the heat and stir in the sesame oil.

NAPA CABBAGE

In comparison to the common round varieties of cabbage, Napa cabbage, also called Chinese cabbage, is delicately mild and terrific eaten raw. The heads are made up of crinkly, thickly veined leaves that are cream colored with light green tips. Buy them when firm and tightly packed.

YIELD: 4 SERVINGS

¼ cup bottled clam juice

2 tablespoons mirin (Japanese rice wine)

1 tablespoon oyster sauce

1 tablespoon low-sodium soy sauce

1 teaspoon cornstarch mixed with 1 teaspoon water

1 tablespoon peanut oil or vegetable oil

1 pound medium shrimp (approximately 20), peeled and deveined

1 cup thinly sliced cabbage, preferably Napa

1 cup snow peas

1 teaspoon grated fresh ginger

1 teaspoon minced garlic

¼ cup dry sherry or chicken stock

Salt and freshly ground black pepper

1 teaspoon sesame oil

Pan-Fried Salmon and Halibut with Apple

YIELD: 4 SERVINGS

SALMON AND HALIBUT

8 tablespoons (1 stick) butter

2 cups flour, for coating

1 tablespoon garlic powder

Salt and freshly ground black pepper

2 large eggs, beaten

2 cups fine dried breadcrumbs or Japanese-style "panko" breadcrumbs

4 (3-ounce) salmon fillets

4 (3-ounce) halibut fillets

1 Granny Smith apple, peeled, cored, cut into fine matchstick-size pieces, and immediately tossed with the juice of ½ lemon

Juice of ½ lemon, plus wedges (for garnish)

4 sprigs fresh tarragon (for garnish)

4 sprigs Fried Parsley Garnish (optional, recipe follows)

FRIED PARSLEY GARNISH

8 large sprigs parsley

2 cups vegetable oil, for deep-frying

Two kinds of fish are always more special than one, and no more difficult to prepare. Crisp apple strips unite the flavors and add even more crunch to the dish.

SALMON AND HALIBUT

Clarify the butter: In a 1-quart saucepan over low heat, bring the butter to a slow boil until it melts and the milk solids separate from the fat, 10 to 15 minutes. When the bubbling almost stops, remove the pan from the heat and let it stand for a few minutes. With a spoon, skim the foam off the top. Slowly pour the clear yellow liquid through a small strainer into a measuring cup; discard the milk solids at the bottom of the pan. Reserve the clarified butter.

On a plate, combine the flour and garlic powder, and season with salt and pepper. Whisk the eggs in a shallow bowl. On a separate plate, spread out the breadcrumbs.

Divide the clarified butter between 2 skillets and place 1 skillet over medium-high heat.

Lightly coat the salmon fillets in the flour and shake off the excess. Dip them into the beaten eggs and then place them in the breadcrumbs to fully coat. When the butter is almost smoking, transfer the salmon to the hot skillet. Cook the salmon until golden brown, 3 to 4 minutes per side.

Repeat with the remaining butter and the halibut fillets in the second skillet.

To serve, place 1 salmon fillet and 1 halibut fillet on each plate. Spoon some apples between them and garnish with lemon wedges, tarragon sprigs, and parsley.

FRIED PARSLEY GARNISH

Gently rinse and thoroughly dry the parsley leaves (placing them on a kitchen towel in front of a fan will dry them faster than a salad spinner).

In a 10-inch frying pan or cast-iron skillet, heat the vegetable oil over medium-high heat until a deep-frying thermometer registers 350°F (do not allow the vegetable oil to smoke). Line a baking sheet with 2 sheets of paper towels.

When the vegetable oil is hot enough, add 4 parsley sprigs and fry until they turn a brilliant green and are crisp, 2 to 3 seconds. With a slotted spoon, carefully transfer the parsley to the prepared baking sheet. Repeat with the remaining parsley sprigs. (Fried parsley should be used quickly or else it will lose its crispness.)

Red Snapper Baked in Parchment

Baking in parchment or "en papillote," is a flexible cooking method and keeps the fish moist and flavorful. And because the baking utensil is paper, clean up is a breeze! If you like, substitute tilapia, catfish, orange roughy, or any firm fish for the snapper. And instead of arugula and tomato, place the fish on a bed of sautéed, sliced vegetables, such as zucchini, carrot, and leek, and spread the fish with a compound butter from Chapter 1. Serve with boiled new potatoes.

Heat the oven to 350°F. Fold each piece of parchment in half and cut into a half heart shape. Set the parchment "hearts" aside.

Heat the olive oil over medium heat in a small skillet. Add the garlic and cook, stirring, until fragrant and softened, about 1 minute. Remove from the heat.

Open a parchment heart on a work surface. Place ½ cup arugula on 1 side of the parchment in an area the size of the fish fillet. Sprinkle some sliced garlic on the arugula.

Season each fish fillet with salt and pepper. Place the fish on the arugula and top with some chopped tomato (or tomato bruschetta) and more garlic. Sprinkle with 1 teaspoon balsamic vinegar and place 2 thyme sprigs on the top.

Fold the parchment over to enclose the fish. Starting at the wider end, crimp the parchment edges to seal. Transfer the fish to a large baking sheet and repeat with the remaining ingredients to make 3 more packages. (The packages can be made 4 hours ahead and kept in the refrigerator.)

Place the baking sheet in the oven and bake for 15 to 18 minutes, or until the parchment is fully puffed. Transfer to 4 plates and serve immediately, allowing each person to open the parchment packet.

YIELD: 4 SERVINGS

4 (15-inch) squares parchment paper

1 tablespoon extra virgin olive oil

4 large cloves garlic, thinly sliced

2 cups baby arugula or spinach leaves

4 (4-ounce) red snapper fillets

Salt and freshly ground black pepper

1½ cups peeled, seeded, and chopped tomato (see page 80) or ¾ cup jarred sun-dried tomato bruschetta topping

4 teaspoons balsamic vinegar

8 sprigs fresh thyme

Seafood Kebabs with Herb Yogurt Dressing

YIELD: 6 SERVINGS

SEAFOOD KEBABS

⅓ cup fresh lemon juice (about 3 lemons)

1 tablespoon Dijon mustard

1 teaspoon minced garlic

¼ teaspoon salt

¼ teaspoon freshly ground black pepper

¼ cup pure olive oil

¼ cup minced fresh dill

¾ pound tuna steak, cut into 1-inch cubes

¾ pound center-cut salmon fillet, cut into 1-inch cubes

¾ pound halibut or skinless swordfish steak, cut into 1-inch cubes

1 large red bell pepper, cored, seeded, and cut into 16 squares

1 red onion, sliced into 1½-inch rings and then cut into squares

6 (10-inch) bamboo or metal skewers

HERB YOGURT DRESSING

8 ounces plain yogurt

1 cup warm water

2 tablespoons fresh lemon juice (about 1 lemon)

1 teaspoon Worcestershire sauce

¼ cup extra virgin olive oil

¼ cup minced fresh flat-leaf parsley

¼ cup minced fresh dill

¼ cup chopped fresh basil

1 tablespoon minced fresh tarragon

Salt and freshly ground black pepper

T he key to success for these kebabs is using the freshest possible fish—and, consequently, being flexible with the kinds you use. If tuna, salmon, or halibut aren't available, try swordfish and shrimp. For added flavor, serve the kebabs with the herb yogurt dressing or with a flavored butter of your own creation.

SEAFOOD KEBABS

In a large glass or stainless steel bowl, combine the lemon juice, mustard, garlic, salt, and pepper. Slowly whisk in the olive oil and then stir in the dill.

Add the tuna, salmon, and halibut cubes; bell peppers; and onions to the lemon juice marinade. Gently toss to lightly coat. Allow to marinate at room temperature for 15 to 30 minutes. While the fish marinates, soak the bamboo skewers, if using, in warm water.

Heat a grill (charcoal, gas, or electric) to medium-high heat. Alternately thread the seafood cubes on the skewers with the bell peppers and onions.

Grill the kebabs, turning occasionally, on an oiled rack set 5 to 6 inches over the heat source until the fish is just opaque in the center and the peppers and onions are slightly charred, 4 to 5 minutes. (Alternatively, you can broil the kebabs under a preheated broiler 3 to 4 inches from the heat element. Broil 4 minutes.)

Transfer the kebabs to a platter. Drizzle with the yogurt dressing and serve immediately.

HERB YOGURT DRESSING

In a glass bowl, combine the yogurt, water, lemon juice, and Worcestershire sauce. Slowly whisk in the olive oil. Stir in the parsley, dill, basil, and tarragon. Season with salt and pepper. Cover and refrigerate until ready to use.

Coconut Seared Scallops

As an accompaniment, try the Mango and Red Bell Pepper Salsa (see page 28), or just serve with your favorite jarred chutney.

Heat the oven to 350°F. Bring the water to a boil in a medium saucepan. Add the coconut, stir once, and then drain in a medium sieve. Transfer the coconut to a plate lined with paper towels and pat dry.

Spread the coconut out in one layer on a baking sheet. Place in the oven and bake, stirring once or twice, for 15 minutes, or until pale golden. Transfer to a bowl and let cool completely. In a food processor or in batches in a coffee grinder, combine the coconut and salt and finely grind; set aside.

Place the flour in a shallow bowl. Beat the egg in a separate shallow bowl. Spread the coconut mixture on a plate.

Season the scallops with salt and cayenne pepper. Lightly coat a scallop with flour and shake off the excess. Dip it into the beaten egg and then in the coconut to fully coat; repeat with the remaining scallops.

In a 10-inch frying pan or cast-iron skillet, heat the vegetable oil over medium-high heat, adding more oil, if necessary, to reach a height of ½ inch in the pan. When the vegetable oil is very hot but not smoking, add just enough scallops to fit comfortably in the pan. Fry until just cooked through and golden brown, about 1½ minutes per side. Drain on a plate lined with paper towels; repeat with the remaining scallops. Serve immediately with salsa or chutney, as desired.

YIELD: 2 SERVINGS

2 cups water

1 cup flaked coconut, sweetened or unsweetened

½ teaspoon salt

1 cup all-purpose flour

1 large egg

10 medium sea scallops (about ½ pound), patted dry and the tough muscle removed from the side of each if necessary

¼ teaspoon cayenne pepper or curry powder

½ cup vegetable or peanut oil plus extra if necessary

Every cuisine on earth offers vegetarian preparations, but generally speaking, most people will categorize a dish by its ethnic origins rather than its status as vegetarian, vegan, or nonvegetarian. Take a look back to the Pasta & Rice chapter and you'll note that half of the recipes are vegetarian. Likewise, in the Salads and Small Bites chapters, there are plenty of recipes that fall naturally under a vegetarian or vegan category. | This book reflects the sensibilities and high standards to which we adhere at Holland America Line. Our menus always offer a minimum of two vegetarian entrées, which are clearly designated as such on the menu. This practice is oft praised by our guests. Vegetarians, of course, appreciate not having to ask for a list of ingredients, and diners who simply crave a meatless meal during their cruise value having a clear choice. | More and more people are training their dietary habits to a vegetarian-inspired model. Increasingly, too, others are converting to a true vegetarian lifestyle. So it's wise when entertaining to have a vegetarian side dish or entrée as part of your menu—or at least on standby. | The vegetarian dishes here are simple to prepare and delightful to eat. All are inspired by Mediterranean cuisine, hailed across the globe as the world's healthiest diet. The fat content in meat and meat stocks impart a great deal of flavor to any dish, so when creating strictly vegetarian recipes it's important to combine powerful flavor ingredients like olives, toasted nuts, herbs and spices with vegetables, and grains and beans to yield delicious and satisfying main courses. | Start with these vegetarian and vegan recipes and consider building up your repertoire of brilliant vegetarian dishes that you would be proud to serve to anyone—vegetarian or otherwise.

CHAPTER 9

VEGETARIAN

Grilled Vegetables with Red Bell Pepper Vinaigrette

YIELD: 2 SERVINGS

RED BELL PEPPER VINAIGRETTE

1 medium red bell pepper, roasted, skinned, and seeded, or ⅓ cup drained bottled roasted red peppers

2 teaspoons balsamic vinegar

1 teaspoon fresh lemon juice

1 tablespoon water

1 tablespoon extra virgin olive oil

1 tablespoon corn oil

¼ teaspoon minced garlic

Salt and freshly ground black pepper

When preparing this colorful collection of grilled vegetables take inspiration from what's in season. Roam the markets and buy what's freshest and most colorful. Other options include eggplant, red onions, portobello mushrooms, asparagus, chayote squash, large carrots sliced diagonally, and even avocado. To play up the southwestern theme, serve the vegetables with flour tortillas and salsa, and top with queso fresco.

RED BELL PEPPER VINAIGRETTE

Use a blender to combine the bell pepper, balsamic vinegar, lemon juice, water, oils, and garlic. Blend until emulsified. Season with salt and pepper.

GRILLED VEGETABLES

Heat a charcoal grill to medium hot (when you can hold your hand 5 inches above the rack for 3 to 4 seconds) or preheat a gas grill to high, covered, for 10 minutes and then reduce the heat to medium. With the flat side of a chef's knife, mash the garlic to a paste on a cutting board with ¼ teaspoon salt; place in a small bowl and whisk with 1 cup corn oil; set aside.

Grill the corn first, turning every 1 or 2 minutes, until tender and lightly golden, about 8 minutes total; remove and let cool slightly. Strip off the charred husks and silk, stand the corn upright on a cutting board,

SKINNING BELL PEPPERS AND CHILES

To skin and seed bell peppers and chiles, lay the peppers and chiles on their sides on the racks of gas burners. Turn the flames on moderately high and roast them, turning frequently with tongs, until the skins are blistered and charred all over. (Alternatively, broil the peppers and chiles on a broiler rack 2 inches from the heat element.) Transfer them immediately to a large bowl and let stand, covered, for 20 minutes. With paper towels, peel or rub off the blackened skins, then remove the seeds and cut as indicated.

and carefully use a sharp knife to cut off the kernels from the middle of the ear to the bottom. Turn over the ear and cut off the remaining kernels in the same way. Place the kernels in a bowl, season with salt and pepper, and set aside.

In a large bowl, combine the zucchini, squash, bell peppers, and tomatoes. Toss with just enough garlic oil to lightly coat. Season with salt and pepper. Grill the zucchini and squash for 8 to 10 minutes, turning once; transfer to a plate. Grill the peppers and tomatoes, in a grill basket or on skewers, until tender and lightly charred, about 8 minutes; transfer to the plate with the zucchini.

Toss the scallions with some garlic oil and season with salt and pepper. Quickly grill the scallions until lightly charred and add to the zucchini.

To serve, spoon 2 to 3 tablespoons of the Red Bell Pepper Vinaigrette onto each plate and arrange the grilled vegetables on top of it. Brush the vegetables with the pesto, if using. Sprinkle with the grilled corn and serve immediately.

See photograph of dish on page 6

GRILLED AVOCADO

When you grill an avocado, the outside turns crispy and the inside molten. It requires a well oiled grill rack to be accomplished neatly, so if your first attempt is less than stellar, you can always just mash the slices in a bowl with some lime juice and seasoning and make smoky guacamole.

Buy a Hass avocado that is just turning soft and not fully ripe, and cut it into ¼-inch-thick slices. Toss the slices with the juice of 1 lime. Brush down the grill rack to clean it and then oil the rack: Fold a piece of paper towel into a pad, dip it into some corn oil, hold it with tongs, and rub it over the rack. Brush the avocado slices with the garlic oil (see Grilled Vegetables recipe) and season with salt and pepper. Grill the avocado slices for 1 minute on each side. You can also grill tomato slices with the same method, but grill for 30 seconds on each side.

GRILLED VEGETABLES

1 teaspoon minced garlic

Salt and freshly ground black pepper

1 cup corn oil plus extra for oiling the grill

2 ears corn, stripped down until just the silk and the innermost layer of husk remain; silk ends at the top snipped off

1 zucchini, no more than 8 inches long, trimmed and sliced lengthwise into ¼- to ½-inch-thick slices

1 yellow squash, trimmed and sliced lengthwise into ¼- to ½-inch-thick slices

3 tricolor bell peppers (1 red, 1 yellow, 1 green), stemmed, seeded, and cut into triangle shapes

6 to 8 cherry tomatoes, yellow or red or a combination

4 scallions, root ends and tough tops trimmed

¼ cup pesto sauce or bottled or homemade basil oil (optional, see page 56)

Sautéed Chard with Cannellini Beans and Caramelized Leeks

This recipe is very adaptable. Try substituting chopped fennel for the leeks, or add thin strips of carrot or chopped fresh tomato. And always remember to include the stems when you cook chard—they are delicious when well seasoned and have a firm texture similar to cooked asparagus.

In a large nonstick skillet, heat the butter over medium heat. Add the leeks and stir to coat. Cover and cook, stirring every 5 minutes, until the leeks are golden brown, about 20 minutes total. Season with sea salt and white pepper; remove from the heat and set aside. (The leeks will keep in the refrigerator, in a covered container, for 1 day.)

Cut the stems from the chard and chop them into ¼-inch-thick pieces; set aside. Stack the chard leaves, roll them into cylinders, and slice them crosswise to make ½-inch-thick strips; set aside separately from the stems.

Heat the olive oil in a large skillet over medium-high heat. Add the garlic and chard stems and cook, stirring occasionally, until the stems are tender, about 5 minutes. Season with sea salt and white pepper.

Add half the chard leaves and all the rosemary to the skillet. Continue to sauté, stirring frequently, until wilted (add a splash of water if they begin to turn brown), about 1 minute. Add the remaining chard leaves and cook, stirring, for 2 minutes more. Add the lemon juice and season with sea salt and white pepper.

Add the beans to the leeks and place over medium heat. Cook, stirring gently, until combined and heated through.

To serve, add the leek mixture to the chard and gently toss to combine. Divide among plates and serve immediately.

YIELD: 4 SERVINGS

3 tablespoons butter

4 medium leeks (white and light green parts only), halved lengthwise, rinsed, and chopped (about 5 cups)

Sea salt (or smoked salt) and freshly ground white pepper

2 (1-pound) bunches Swiss chard or rainbow chard

2 tablespoons extra virgin olive oil

2 teaspoons minced garlic

½ teaspoon minced fresh rosemary

2 teaspoons fresh lemon juice

2 (14- to 15-ounce) cans cannellini beans, drained and rinsed

Tower of Roasted Vegetables with Mozzarella and Tomato Sauce

YIELD: 2 SERVINGS

1 small purple eggplant, to make
2 to 4 slices of the same diameter
as the mozzarella

1 zucchini, cut crosswise into
¼-inch-thick slices

1 yellow squash, cut crosswise into
¼-inch-thick slices

2 tablespoons extra virgin olive oil
plus extra for brushing

Salt and freshly ground black pepper

Basil oil (optional, for drizzling; see
page 56)

1 (8-ounce) ball fresh, water-packed
mozzarella cheese, cut into 10 slices

1 large ripe red tomato, sliced into
2 to 4 slices

2 sprigs fresh rosemary (for garnish)

½ cup Basic Tomato Sauce
(see page 22)

M ake this during the peak of late summer, when eggplant, tomato, and squash varieties abound. Buy the ball of mozzarella first, then choose a tomato and eggplant of a matching diameter. The zucchini and yellow squash can be slender—three or four slices can make up a single layer. If you like, serve with arugula quick-sautéed with balsamic vinaigrette or roasted asparagus spears (which can roast alongside the vegetable towers).

In a large bowl, combine the slices of eggplant, zucchini, and yellow squash. Toss with 2 tablespoons olive oil and season with salt and pepper.

Heat a charcoal grill to medium hot (when you can hold your hand 5 inches above the rack for 3 to 4 seconds) or heat a grill pan over high heat. Grill the eggplant slices until well-marked by the grill and softened, about 3 minutes per side. Transfer to a large plate and grill the zucchini and yellow squash in the same manner (use a grill basket, if you have one, for the charcoal grill). Drizzle the vegetables very lightly with a small amount of basil oil, if using. Let them cool to room temperature.

Heat the oven to 400°F. Place two 5-inch squares of foil on a baking sheet and brush them with olive oil. Make 2 towers using alternating layers of tomato, mozzarella, zucchini, eggplant, and yellow squash in any pattern you like (several slightly overlapping squash circles can make up a single layer). Place a skewer through the center of each tower down to the base to keep it in place (the skewer will stay in place throughout the cooking).

Place the baking sheet in the oven and roast the towers for 15 minutes (keep checking so that the mozzarella doesn't burn).

Use the skewer to help you transfer each tower to a plate, sliding it off the foil right before positioning. Remove the skewer and place a sprig of rosemary in its place. Spoon some tomato sauce on and around each tower and serve immediately.

Couscous Salad with Roasted Squash and Apricots

This main-course salad, served at room temperature, just sings with spices. It's filling on its own or makes a great companion to grilled chicken.

Heat the oven to 400°F. In a large bowl, combine the zucchini, yellow squash, bell pepper, and scallions. Toss with 3 tablespoons olive oil and season with salt and pepper. Divide the vegetables between 2 heavy baking sheets and roast on separate racks for 45 minutes, or until tender, switching places in the oven halfway through and turning once. Set aside.

Heat 2 tablespoons olive oil in a large saucepan over medium heat. Add the onion and cook, stirring, until tender and aromatic, 3 to 5 minutes. Stir in the cumin, turmeric, nutmeg, and ginger. Season with salt and pepper. Cook, stirring, for 1 minute more. Add the broth and bring just to a boil. Slowly add the couscous, stirring constantly, then remove the pan from the heat and stir in the fresh apricots and chickpeas. Cover the pan and set aside for 15 minutes. Transfer the couscous mixture to a large bowl and fluff with a fork.

Meanwhile, toast the almonds: In a dry heavy skillet over medium-high heat, toss or stir the almonds until lightly browned, 3 to 4 minutes; set aside.

Add the vegetables to the couscous along with the parsley and gently stir to combine. In a small bowl, whisk the lemon juice with the remaining 4 tablespoons olive oil and pour the mixture over the couscous, tossing evenly to coat. Season with salt and pepper. (The couscous salad can be stored, covered, in the refrigerator for up to 6 hours. Serve cold or at room temperature.)

Divide the couscous among serving plates and sprinkle with the almonds.

YIELD: 4 SERVINGS

2 medium zucchini, cut in half lengthwise and crosswise into ½-inch slices

2 medium yellow squash, cut in half lengthwise and crosswise into ½-inch slices

1 red bell pepper, cut into ½-inch-wide strips

6 scallions, white and light green parts only, cut into 1½-inch lengths

9 tablespoons extra virgin olive oil, divided

Salt and freshly ground black pepper

½ medium onion, finely chopped

1 teaspoon ground cumin

½ teaspoon turmeric

¼ teaspoon freshly grated nutmeg

¼ teaspoon ground ginger

3 cups store-bought vegetable broth

1 (10-ounce) box instant couscous (about 1⅔ cups)

4 to 6 fresh apricots or ¾ cup dried apricots, diced

1 (15½-ounce) can chickpeas, rinsed and well drained

½ cup sliced almonds

¼ cup finely chopped flat-leaf parsley

⅓ cup fresh lemon juice

Red Bell Peppers Stuffed with Barley and Provençal Vegetables

1 large red vine-ripened tomato, seeded and finely chopped

½ cup pitted niçoise olives, finely chopped

1 tablespoon minced fresh thyme or 1½ teaspoons dried thyme

1 tablespoon minced fresh oregano or 1½ teaspoons dried oregano

1 tablespoon minced fresh chives or flat-leaf parsley

1 teaspoon ground coriander

½ cup (about 8 tablespoons) extra virgin olive oil, divided

2 tablespoons butter

½ cup minced onion

1 tablespoon minced garlic

1 cup quick-cooking barley, prepared according to package instructions, or 3 cups cooked barley

Salt and freshly ground black pepper

4 medium-size red bell peppers (each about 4 to 6 ounces), halved lengthwise and seeded

¼ cup prepared black olive tapenade (olive paste), jarred sun-dried tomato bruschetta topping, or homemade Sun-Dried Tomato Pesto (for garnish, see page 21)

½ cup alfalfa sprouts (for garnish)

The rustic filling would also work beautifully as a stuffing in meaty portobello mushrooms, just remove the stems and gills.

Heat the oven to 425°F. Combine the tomato, olives, thyme, oregano, chives, and coriander in a large bowl. Toss with 2 tablespoons olive oil and set aside briefly for the flavors to combine.

Heat the butter over medium heat in a large heavy skillet. Add the onion and cook, stirring, until translucent, about 3 minutes. Add the garlic and cook, stirring, for 30 seconds more. Add the barley and toss to combine. With a heat-proof rubber spatula, scrape the barley mixture into the bowl with the tomato mixture and gently toss. Season with salt and pepper.

In a large bowl, toss the bell pepper halves with 2 tablespoons olive oil. Season with salt and pepper. One by one, fill the pepper halves with the barley mixture, mounding slightly. Arrange the peppers in a 9-by-13-by-2-inch baking dish. (The dish can be made up to this point 1 day in advance and stored, covered, in the refrigerator.)

Drizzle the peppers with 2 tablespoons olive oil and bake for 10 to 15 minutes, or until the peppers are soft and the filling is heated through. Meanwhile, in a small bowl whisk together the black olive tapenade with the remaining 2 tablespoons olive oil. Divide the peppers among 4 plates and serve with some tapenade sauce on each plate. Garnish with alfalfa sprouts and serve immediately.

Vegetable Tagine with Almond Couscous

T his tagine takes well to improvisation—chopped fresh tomatoes, cubed butternut squash, cauliflower florets, button mushrooms, sweet potato, and yellow squash all make fine additions or substitutions.

Heat the olive oil in a soup pot over medium-high heat. Add the onion, garlic, zucchini, carrots, and eggplant. Cook, stirring, for 5 minutes. Add the green beans, cumin, paprika, ginger, and vegetable broth. Bring to a boil. Reduce the heat to low and simmer, covered, until all the vegetables are cooked, 10 to 15 minutes.

Meanwhile, cook the couscous according to the package instructions. Toast the almonds: In a dry heavy skillet over medium-high heat, toss or stir the almonds until lightly browned, 3 to 4 minutes; set aside.

Add the chickpeas, prunes, and ¼ cup parsley to the simmering vegetables and cook until heated through (add more vegetable broth if the mixture is becoming too dry). Season with salt and pepper.

Stir the remaining ¼ cup parsley into the couscous and divide it among serving plates; sprinkle with the almonds. Spoon the tagine alongside and serve immediately.

YIELD: 4 SERVINGS

2 tablespoons pure olive oil

1 large onion, diced

2 teaspoons minced garlic

2 medium zucchini, trimmed and diced

3 medium carrots, diced

1 small eggplant or 2 Japanese eggplants, diced (about 1½ cups)

1 cup green beans, trimmed

½ teaspoon ground cumin

½ teaspoon paprika

2 teaspoons minced fresh ginger

2 cups store-bought vegetable broth, plus extra as needed

1 (12-ounce) box instant couscous

¼ cup sliced almonds

1 (15-ounce) can chickpeas (or garbanzo beans), drained

½ cup pitted prunes

½ cup chopped fresh flat-leaf parsley, divided

Salt and freshly ground black pepper

After the first courses of a truly extraordinary meal, the expectations run high that dessert will at least match if not top all that preceded it. At Holland America Line, we endeavor to exceed this common human expectation and develop dessert offerings aimed at blowing our guests out of the water. │ Dessert is arguably the highlight of any evening spent at a table. But that doesn't mean that a dessert has to be complicated to make to be a sublime ending to an elegant meal. │ Here we have several very simple recipes for those wonderful times when you can get beautiful full-colored fruit in season. Berries with a simple lemon mint syrup served in a delicately stemmed wine glass, or in a shot glass for fun, are a wonderful choice—a punctuation of refreshing sweetness in the summer's heat. │ Fruit desserts at Holland America Line are in especially high demand on our cruises to and through the Caribbean, Hawaii, Panama Canal, Mexico, Australia, New Zealand, and the South Pacific. Desserts like the Vanilla Ice Cream with Spicy Pineapple Salsa and Quick Buñuelos bring exotic island flavors right to the table. On a trip to Europe you will encounter a dessert like Salzburger Nockerln—a dream of a dessert that, when prepared correctly, defies both gravity and imagination. Here there is something to suit every taste, from warm desserts, such as the Chocolate and Raisin Bread Pudding and Strawberry Rhubarb Crisp, to no-fail chilled favorites like Chocolate Mousse Espresso. Having the recipe for your dessert printed out on a heavy-stock paper would make a lovely gift for dinner-party guests. If the way these desserts are received aboard a Holland America cruise is any indication, every guest at your table will ask how you made whichever sweet you choose.

CHAPTER 10

DESSERTS

Berries with Lemon Mint Syrup

YIELD: 4 SERVINGS

1½ cups water

¾ cup sugar

1 cup firmly packed mint leaves and tender stems, crushed, plus 4 sprigs extra (for garnish)

Zest from 1 lemon, cut off in ½-inch-wide strips, remove any bitter white pith attached

1½ quarts mixed berries, such as blueberries, raspberries, blackberries, and quartered strawberries

This fruit dessert is easy to prepare and a wonderful way to highlight the ripest of berries. The berries and lemon mint syrup are a summery, satisfying close to any dinner.

In a medium saucepan, combine the water, sugar, mint leaves and stems, and lemon zest. Bring to a boil over medium-high heat. As soon as it boils, remove from the heat and let stand, covered, for 20 minutes. Strain the syrup into a larger saucepan.

Bring the syrup back to a simmer. Remove from the heat and add the berries. Stir gently and then pour the mixture into a glass or ceramic bowl. Let cool to room temperature. Ladle the berries and syrup into serving bowls and top with fresh mint sprigs.

Peach and Raspberry Trifle

This dessert comes together quickly if you buy good-quality angel food cake.

In a small bowl, combine 1 cup raspberries and 3 tablespoons sugar. With a fork, crush the berries to incorporate the sugar; let stand at room temperature for 1 hour.

With a rubber spatula, press the raspberry/sugar mixture through a fine strainer set over a bowl until only the seeds remain in the strainer; discard the seeds. Add the remaining 2 cups raspberries to the strained purée and gently toss to combine.

Roughly mash the peaches either by placing them in a bowl and using a potato masher or processing them quickly in a food processor. Transfer the peaches to a bowl. Taste for sweetness and add up to 3 tablespoons brown sugar.

In a small bowl, combine the sour cream and heavy cream.

To assemble the trifle, spoon some raspberry mixture in the bottom of a 2½-quart glass bowl or attractive serving dish. Fit some cake pieces in a single layer over the raspberries. Cover the cake layer with a quarter of the remaining raspberry mixture, a quarter of the peaches, and finally a quarter of the cream mixture. Repeat layering all the ingredients 3 more times, finishing with the cream mixture. (There may be a little cake left over.)

Cover the trifle with plastic wrap and refrigerate for at least several hours before serving.

YIELD: 10 SERVINGS

3 cups fresh raspberries

3 tablespoons sugar

8 large peaches, peeled, pitted, and cut into 1-inch slices

3 tablespoons brown sugar

2 cups sour cream

¼ cup heavy cream

1 prepared plain angel food cake, cut into 1-inch cubes

Strawberry Rhubarb Crisp

YIELD: 6 TO 8 SERVINGS

TOPPING

1½ cups all-purpose flour

1 cup sugar

½ teaspoon salt

¼ teaspoon nutmeg

11 tablespoons chilled butter, cut into ¼-inch pieces

FILLING

3½ cups diced rhubarb, trimmed

2½ cups diced strawberries

¾ cup sugar

3 tablespoons all-purpose flour

Because many factors affect baking time, including the size of your oven, it's important to start checking the crisp after 20 minutes to make sure the topping doesn't burn. Serve warm with ice cream and, for added elegance, drizzle with a good-quality bottled strawberry fruit syrup.

TOPPING

Heat the oven to 425°F. In a food processor, blend the flour, sugar, salt, and nutmeg until just combined. Pulse in the butter, using on/off turns, until moist clumps form. (Alternatively, in a medium bowl combine the flour, sugar, salt, and nutmeg. Add the butter, rubbing it in with your fingertips or with a pastry blender until the topping holds together in small moist clumps.)

Set the topping aside. The topping can be made in advance, covered, and refrigerated for up to 3 days.

FILLING

Combine all the ingredients in a large glass or ceramic bowl, and toss gently with a rubber spatula. Transfer to a 9-inch glass pie pan or other baking pan, allowing the fruit to mound slightly.

Carefully place the topping on the fruit, spreading it evenly over the surface with your hands. Press down gently to compact it.

Put the pan on a baking sheet and bake in the oven for 35 to 45 minutes, or until the top is crisp and the juices just start to bubble around the edge. Transfer to a wire rack and let cool for at least 30 minutes before serving.

Phyllo Tartlets with Strawberries and Cinnamon-Mascarpone Cream

YIELD: 6 SERVINGS

CINNAMON-MASCARPONE CREAM

¼ cup mascarpone cheese

½ cup sour cream

Grated zest of 2 oranges, juice of 1 orange

Grated zest of 1 lime

1 tablespoon vanilla extract

3 tablespoons sugar

1 teaspoon cinnamon

PHYLLO AND STRAWBERRIES

4 sheets frozen phyllo dough (18- by 14-inches), thawed

4 tablespoons butter, melted

5 tablespoons sugar, divided

2 pints strawberries, washed, trimmed, and sliced

1 tablespoon balsamic vinegar

Confectioners' sugar, for sprinkling

Here, an appealing contrast of flavors and textures produces a dessert that is both lovely and delicious. For the best flavor and texture, make the cinnamon-mascarpone cream one day in advance. The phyllo rectangles can be baked in advance, too, and stored well-covered to remain crisp.

CINNAMON-MASCARPONE CREAM

Whisk all the ingredients in a glass or ceramic bowl. Cover with plastic wrap and chill overnight to firm up and allow the flavors to blend.

PHYLLO AND STRAWBERRIES

Heat the oven to 350°F. Lay 1 sheet of phyllo on a sheet of parchment paper or a Silpat. (Keep remaining phyllo covered with a damp kitchen towel and plastic wrap.) With a pastry brush, lightly brush the phyllo sheet with some melted butter. Sprinkle 1 tablespoon sugar evenly over the whole surface. Repeat the process with the remaining 3 sheets of phyllo, stacking each sheet on top of the one before it and brushing with butter and sprinkling with 1 tablespoon sugar.

Transfer the parchment or Silpat with the phyllo to a baking sheet. With a knife or pizza cutter, cut 2-by-3-inch squares. Top with another sheet of parchment and nestle another sheet pan on top to keep the phyllo pressed down while baking. Bake for 10 to 12 minutes, or until crisp and golden brown. Cool on a wire rack and store the rectangles in a covered container until ready to use.

In a glass or ceramic bowl, toss the strawberries with the remaining 1 tablespoon sugar and the balsamic vinegar. To assemble, place a phyllo rectangle on a plate, top with some cinnamon-mascarpone cream and some strawberries. Top with another phyllo rectangle, more cream, and more berries. Finish with a phyllo rectangle and sprinkle with confectioners' sugar. Make 5 more stacks with the remaining ingredients and serve immediately.

Mango Mousse with Strawberries

2 pounds mangoes, peeled, pitted, and diced (see page 63) or 1 pound frozen mango chunks

1½ cups sugar

1 cinnamon stick

Juice of 1 lime

4 tablespoons (½ stick) butter, melted

3 tablespoons (3 envelopes) unflavored gelatin

½ cup whole milk

2 cups fresh whipped cream (from 8 ounces heavy whipping cream) or whipped topping

3 large egg whites (see page 65 for information about raw eggs)

1 pint strawberries, hulled and sliced (for garnish)

Buy an extra mango if you want to garnish the mousse with diced mango, to make this a three-way mango extravaganza.

Make the mango purée: In a saucepan, combine the mango, sugar, cinnamon stick, and lime juice over medium heat. Cook, stirring, until the mango juices and sugar create a syrup, about 20 minutes. Remove from the heat and allow the mixture to cool. Transfer to a blender and purée until smooth. Store, covered, in the refrigerator until ready to use.

On a piece of parchment or waxed paper, trace and cut out 10 circles the size of the bottom of ramekins. Brush the insides of 10 ramekins with the butter and place one circle in each ramekin. Brush each circle with more melted butter.

In a small bowl, combine the gelatin and milk and let it sit for 5 minutes. Place in the microwave for 30 seconds to melt the gelatin, making sure there are no lumps (if there are lumps, microwave for a few more seconds). Allow the gelatin mixture to come to room temperature—it should not be hot before you proceed.

Measure out 3 cups mango purée into a large bowl. Whisk in the room-temperature gelatin mixture. With a rubber spatula, fold in the whipped cream.

In a clean bowl whip the egg whites with an electric mixer on high speed until stiff peaks form. With a rubber spatula, gently fold the egg whites into the mango mixture.

Fill the prepared ramekins with the mango mixture, cover, and chill in the refrigerator for at least 2 hours. Unmold each mousse onto dessert plates and serve with the remaining mango purée, chopped mango, and sliced strawberries.

Mixed Fruit Salad with Sweet Tahini Yogurt

For a taste of the tropics, substitute lychees (fresh or canned) for the blueberries and raspberries and garnish the salads with slices of fresh star fruit.

Whisk together the yogurt, honey, and tahini in a glass or ceramic bowl. Cover and store in the refrigerator until needed.

In a large bowl, gently combine the mango, pineapple, grapes, grapefruit, blueberries, and raspberries. Divide the fruit among the bowls and top each with some of the tahini yogurt sauce. Garnish with the pineapple leaves and serve immediately.

YIELD: 4 TO 6 SERVINGS

1 cup full-fat Greek yogurt or other thick imported yogurt

1½ tablespoons honey

1½ tablespoons well-stirred tahini (Middle Eastern sesame paste)

½ cup diced fresh mango

½ cup diced fresh pineapple

½ cup red seedless grapes, sliced in half lengthwise

½ cup green seedless grapes, sliced in half lengthwise

1 grapefruit, segmented, tough membranes removed

½ cup blueberries

½ cup raspberries

4 to 6 small inner leaves from the top of a fresh pineapple (for garnish)

Vanilla Ice Cream with Spicy Pineapple Salsa and Quick Buñuelos

YIELD: 4 TO 6 SERVINGS

1 (20-ounce) can unsweetened pineapple tidbits or chunks, with juice

4 fresh mint leaves, halved

1 tablespoon finely chopped red chili pepper

3 tablespoons confectioners' sugar

¾ teaspoon ground cinnamon

2 cups vegetable oil, for deep-frying

5 (8-inch) flour tortillas, cut into 8 wedges each

1 quart vanilla ice cream

When deep-fried, flour tortillas puff up and become crisp. Sprinkled with cinnamon and sugar, they turn pastrylike and make a terrific accompaniment to ice cream and spicy fruit salsa.

To make the pineapple salsa: Combine the pineapple, mint, and chili pepper in a small saucepan set over medium heat. Simmer, uncovered, for about 5 minutes. Remove from the heat and cool thoroughly. Remove the mint. Cover and store in the refrigerator until ready to serve.

Combine the sugar and cinnamon in a small bowl; set aside.

HOW TO DEEP-FRY

When deep-frying, it's important to use enough oil so that the food is at least partially submerged. It's also important to use an easy-to-read digital thermometer to keep tabs on the temperature, which can fluctuate as you add or remove items from the oil. Depending on the recipe, foods are fried at between 325 and 375°F. If the temperature of the oil goes so high that it starts to smoke, the oil has begun the process of breaking down and will develop unpleasant flavors that will transfer to the food. You should discard that oil and start again with fresh oil. If the temperature is too low, the food will need to remain in the oil too long to turn crisp and will soak up too much oil and taste greasy. Foods fried at the correct temperature develop a crispy crust and spend less time in the oil.

For deep-frying small items quickly, use canola or vegetable oil. They have high smoke points and almost no flavor. However, they begin to break down and produce off flavors after about 15 minutes, so when deep-frying items such as chicken and French fries, which take more time to cook, use refined peanut oil instead. It has a neutral flavor but doesn't break down, even at high temperatures held longer than 15 minutes.

Peanut oil used for deep-frying nonprotein items such as French fries, tortillas, or doughnuts can be reused as long as it has been preserved intact as much as possible. To do that, don't let the oil reach the smoke point and eliminate the introduction of water and salt to the oil by patting dry the food before frying and seasoning only after the frying is done. In addition, remove bits of food by straining the oil through a paper coffee filter. The smoke point lowers with each successive reuse of oil, so after 3 or 4 uses it will need to be discarded. If you are deep-frying breaded items, a simple way to discard the oil is to pour all the leftover breading mixture, flour, and egg mixture into the pan to absorb the oil, and then when it's cool scrape it into the garbage.

In a 10- or 12-inch frying pan or cast-iron skillet, heat the vegetable oil over medium-high heat until a deep-frying thermometer registers 350°F (do not allow the vegetable oil to smoke). Line a baking sheet with 2 or 3 sheets of paper towels.

Add a handful or two of the tortilla wedges, being careful not to overcrowd the pan, and fry until just crisp, 1 to 2 minutes per side. With a slotted spoon, carefully transfer the tortillas to the paper-towel-lined baking sheet. Sprinkle with generous amounts of the cinnamon-sugar mixture. Repeat with the remaining tortilla wedges, checking the vegetable oil temperature in between batches and adjusting the heat accordingly. (The buñuelos can be stored at room temperature in an airtight container for up to 7 days.)

To serve, place 2 scoops of vanilla ice cream into each bowl and top with some pineapple salsa. Garnish with a few buñuelos and serve immediately.

Salzburger Nockerln

YIELD: 4 TO 6 SERVINGS

6 tablespoons butter, plus extra for buttering the dish

¼ cup orange marmalade or seedless raspberry preserves

4 tablespoons Grand Marnier

8 large egg whites

¼ teaspoon cream of tartar

⅓ cup sugar

4 large egg yolks

3 tablespoons twice-sifted flour

Confectioners' sugar (for garnish)

This is the favorite dessert of Holland America Line president and chief executive officer Stein Kruse, who loves to make this dish for his beautiful family—wife Linda, daughter Victoria, and son Alexander. Famous in Austria, this dessert should be called the "loved for life soufflé" because that's just how long you'll be adored by those for whom you make it. The three mounds represent the three snowy hills, called *nockerln*, that surround the beautiful town of Salzburg. To get the whites to whip high enough, make sure you start with impeccably clean bowls and beaters. Serve this straight out of the oven sprinkled with powdered sugar and fresh berries, if you like.

Heat the oven to 425°F. Butter a 2-quart gratin dish or 7-by-11-inch baking dish. In a small saucepan, combine the 6 tablespoons butter, marmalade, and Grand Marnier. Stir until the butter is melted and everything is combined. Spread the mixture onto the buttered gratin dish. Set aside.

Place the egg whites in the very clean bowl of an electric mixer fitted with the whisk attachment, or in a large mixing bowl. Put the gratin dish in the oven to heat up while you beat the whites (don't let the marmalade mixture burn). With the electric mixer or a hand mixer, beat the egg whites on medium speed just until foamy, about 30 seconds. Add the cream of tartar and continue to beat on medium speed while you slowly sprinkle in the sugar. Continue beating until the whites form stiff peaks.

In a small bowl, lightly beat the egg yolks just until they are broken up and smooth. Put the flour in a small sieve and place on a plate. Using a rubber spatula, very gently fold the egg yolks into the egg whites while simultaneously sprinkling the flour over the mixture as you fold. (The entire process should be done gently but take no more than 10 seconds—if possible, ask someone to sprinkle the flour for you.)

Carefully remove the hot gratin dish from the oven and spoon 3 equal mounds of the soufflé mixture over the hot marmalade, quickly shaping to resemble the 3 mountains of Salzburg. Immediately return the dish to the oven and bake for 8 to 10 minutes, without peeking, until the soufflé is puffed and golden. Immediately sprinkle the confectioners' sugar through a sieve over the soufflé and serve right from the gratin dish, if possible; this soufflé waits for no one!

Key Lime and White Chocolate Tart

YIELD: 12 SERVINGS

8 large egg yolks

1 cup sugar

⅔ cup Key lime juice, fresh or bottled

4 ounces white chocolate, finely chopped

8 tablespoons (1 stick) butter, cut into 16 pieces, at room temperature

1 prebaked 9-inch tart shell or 12 (3-inch) tart shells, baked and cooled

T o save time I recommend using prebaked tart shells, but the recipe certainly can be made with homemade. Either way, the tart's lime-chocolate flavor combination will certainly have your dinner guests asking for more.

Whisk the egg yolks and sugar until smooth in a heavy medium saucepan. Add the Key lime juice and whisk again. Make sure the white chocolate is chopped and ready in a bowl.

Place the saucepan over low heat and cook, stirring constantly with a heat-proof rubber spatula, until the mixture thickens. When you notice the very first bubble of a boil, immediately remove the mixture from the heat and add the white chocolate, stirring until smooth. Stir in the butter, 1 piece at a time, until completely smooth and incorporated.

Pour the mixture into the baked tart shell and smooth out the surface. Chill for 4 hours, or until set. Let stand at room temperature for 30 minutes before serving. To store, cover with plastic wrap and refrigerate.

Chocolate Mousse Espresso

YIELD: 8 SERVINGS

5 ounces bittersweet (*not* unsweetened) chocolate, chopped

1¼ cups heavy cream, plus extra for serving

¾ cup brewed espresso coffee, chilled

2 teaspoons very finely grated orange zest

Semisweet or bittersweet chocolate shavings (for garnish)

C hocolate and coffee are a winning combination and are delicious in this easy-to-make mousse. Use good-quality chocolate and espresso for the best results.

Place the chocolate in the top of a double boiler placed over 1 inch of simmering (not boiling) water. Whisk until the chocolate is smooth and no small lumps remain. Remove the pan from the heat and let cool completely. Set aside.

In a large, chilled mixing bowl, whip 1¼ cups heavy cream until stiff but still glossy. Gradually whip in the espresso and orange zest.

With a rubber spatula, fold the reserved chocolate into the whipped cream. Divide the mousse between 8 glass bowls. Top with more whipped cream, if desired, and chocolate shavings.

Chocolate Zabaglione Sauce with Ice Cream and Raspberries

This elegant sauce is also delicious served over strawberries or cake. It's best made just before you serve it.

YIELD: 4 SERVINGS

3 ounces semisweet chocolate, chopped

6 large egg yolks, at room temperature

¼ cup dry marsala or champagne

½ cup granulated sugar

12 ounces raspberries

4 scoops vanilla ice cream

Put the chocolate in the top of a double boiler placed over 1 inch of simmering (not boiling) water. Whisk until the chocolate is smooth and no small lumps remain. Turn off the heat and remove the chocolate from the hot water. Set aside.

In a wide saucepan, bring about 1 inch of water to a simmer. Adjust the heat so that the water is at a bare simmer. Combine the egg yolks, marsala, and sugar in a large heat-proof mixing bowl (the bowl will need to be big enough to sit on the pan). With an electric mixer, beat until pale in color, stopping 2 or 3 times to scrape down the sides.

Set the bowl over the pan of simmering water and whisk constantly until the mixture thickens and is lemon colored, about 10 minutes. Remove the bowl from the heat. With a rubber spatula, slowly fold the melted chocolate into the egg mixture.

Divide the raspberries among serving dishes. Top the raspberries with the ice cream. Pour the warm zabaglione sauce over the ice cream and serve immediately.

Chocolate and Raisin Bread Pudding

This delectable bread pudding is studded with plump golden raisins and pockets of melted chocolate. The for-adults-only whiskey sauce takes this over the top, but can be replaced with sweetened whipped cream or even vanilla ice cream for the younger set.

WHISKEY SAUCE

In a heavy 2-quart saucepan, heat the cream over medium heat until it boils. In a small bowl, whisk the cornstarch and water; whisk this mixture into the boiling cream.

Return the cream to a boil then reduce the heat to low and cook, stirring with a heat-proof rubber spatula, for 30 seconds, taking care not to let the mixture burn. Add the sugar and whiskey and stir until the sugar is dissolved. Immediately remove from the heat and let cool to room temperature. (Cover and store in the refrigerator until ready to use. Rewarm before serving.)

BREAD PUDDING

Heat the oven to 350°F. Grease a 12-cup muffin tin or a 13-by-9-by-2-inch baking pan to make one. Combine the raisins and whiskey in a small bowl; let sit for at least 15 minutes.

Bring a large kettle of water to a boil. Drain the raisins and discard the liquid. Divide the bread, chocolate chips, and drained raisins among the muffin cups (or place in the baking pan).

In a large bowl, combine the eggs, milk, sugar, cocoa powder, vanilla, and salt. Whisk to blend thoroughly. Pour the egg mixture over the bread in each of the muffin cups (or in the baking pan) and place the pan in a larger roasting pan. Transfer the roasting pan to the oven and add enough boiling water to the larger pan to reach halfway up the side of the muffin or baking pan. Bake the puddings for 30 to 40 minutes (45 minutes to one hour if you make one), or until puffed and just set. Carefully remove the roasting pan from the oven and remove the muffin (or baking) pan inside it. Let the bread pudding cool until warm and serve, unmolded, with the whiskey sauce or the whipped cream and vanilla ice cream (or serve the single bread pudding in the baking pan with the accompaniments).

YIELD: 10 TO 12 SERVINGS

WHISKEY SAUCE

1½ cups heavy cream

2 teaspoons cornstarch

2 tablespoons cold water

⅓ cup sugar

2 tablespoons whiskey, such as Jack Daniels, Jameson, or Old Bushmills

BREAD PUDDING

½ cup golden raisins

2 tablespoons whiskey (for soaking the raisins; optional)

1 pound loaf day-old Italian bread, cut into 1-inch cubes

½ cup semisweet chocolate chips

6 large eggs

1 quart whole milk

1 cup sugar

3 tablespoons unsweetened cocoa powder, sifted

1½ teaspoons vanilla

¼ teaspoon salt

Mascarpone-Filled Poached Pears with Chocolate and Strawberry Sauces

YIELD: 4 SERVINGS

POACHED PEARS

3 oranges

1 small lemon, halved

6 cups water

1½ cups sugar

4 firm but ripe Anjou or Bosc pears

MASCARPONE AND SAUCE

¾ cup heavy cream

⅛ cup dark corn syrup

8 ounces bitter- or semisweet chocolate, chopped

2 tablespoons (¼ stick) butter, softened, divided

¼ cup mascarpone cheese

2 tablespoons confectioners' sugar

Grated zest of 1 orange

1 teaspoon honey

½ cup good-quality bottled strawberry fruit syrup

4 large strawberries, hulled and thinly sliced (for garnish)

4 sprigs mint (for garnish)

While the preparation of this dessert might take a bit longer, the effort pays off with a dish that not only looks impressive but tastes delicious, too.

POACHED PEARS

With a vegetable peeler, remove the zest of the oranges in strips leaving behind any white pith. Squeeze the juice from the oranges into a stainless steel saucepan and add the orange zest, lemon halves (juice squeezed into saucepan), water, and sugar.

Peel the pears, leaving the stems attached, and then hollow them out: At the bottom of the pear, cut out a small amount with a paring knife and continue digging upward with an espresso spoon or melon baller until all of the core is removed and a cavity remains in its place.

Add the pears to the saucepan and place over medium heat. Bring to a simmer, reduce the heat, and continue to simmer for 15 to 20 minutes (depending on the firmness of the pears), or until just tender but not mushy. Remove from the heat and let the pears cool in their liquid, where they will continue to cook a bit. (The pears will keep, covered, in the refrigerator in their poaching liquid, for up to 1 day.)

MASCARPONE AND SAUCE

To make the sauce: In a medium saucepan, bring the heavy cream and corn syrup to a simmer. Remove from the heat and add the chocolate, whisking until smooth. Whisk in 1 tablespoon butter. Let the sauce stand for at least 20 minutes before serving. (The sauce can be stored, covered, in the refrigerator for up to 3 days. Rewarm just before serving.)

To make the filling: In a small bowl, whisk together the mascarpone, sugar, orange zest, honey, and remaining 1 tablespoon butter.

To serve: When the pears are cool enough to handle, stuff the mascarpone mixture into the cavity of the pears using a piping bag or a teaspoon. Place the pears on serving plates and drizzle with the chocolate sauce and strawberry sauce and garnish with the sliced strawberries and mint leaves.

ACKNOWLEDGMENTS

I have a dear friend who says a grace of thanksgiving each evening before dinner. After the short prayer, the youngest member of my friend's family, Liam, says: "And God bless the cook!" Everyone at table lifts a glass and repeats, "God bless the cook!"

Indeed.

I'd like to thank the many cooks who have blessed me with their various talents to help produce the feast that is this book.

I am deeply grateful to Johan Groothuizen, vice president, marine hotel operations, for his commitment to putting Holland America Line's recipes into print. Johan was in no small measure responsible for pushing forward the first-ever Holland America Line cookbook (Rizzoli, 2006), and was likewise instrumental in making this second volume in the series possible.

I'd like to acknowledge all the members of the Holland America Line culinary department as well as the marine hotel department. I am proud to serve with you and thank you all for your willingness to work as a true team to embrace excellence and create new culinary concepts. This book is a tribute to you for the great pride you take in the work you do.

A special shoutout goes to Holland America Line's senior culinary trainer, Executive Chef John Mulvany, with whom I have had the pleasure of working side by side: thank you for the humor, passion, and dedication you always bring to our work together. Likewise, I'd like to acknowledge the hard work of two special senior executive chefs: Eberhard Schmidt and Andreas Summerfeld. A hearty thanks as well goes to Jan Willem Kuipers, manager marine hotel, who was very helpful coordinating schedules and the production of *A Taste of Elegance*.

To Monica Velgos, my recipe editor, who meticulously checks each recipe again and again in the process of our countless revisions: you are a saint and my guardian angel. I cannot imagine what I would do without Monica's keen mind, sharp eye, and endless resourcefulness. Monica's work editing recipes, including writing all the notes and techniques, is second to none. Also, Monica, I applaud you for the care you have for every reader; you work tirelessly so the reader may always succeed in his or her kitchen.

Bravo and deep thanks to my photographers Herb Schmitz and Pat Doyle. You have done it again! You transfer the excitement you generate while you're working behind the lens into each and every stunning photograph. As you say: "It's all in the eye." I am extremely grateful to you both for teaching me the skills I needed to become a good photographer myself. Your energy and enthusiasm for creating beautiful things, your eye for detail, and your commitment to creative integrity inspire the artistry in all the work I do—in front of the lens, and behind it.

To Marcelle Langan DiFalco: your gift for translating the content of my busy mind into words that are a joy to read is a gift to me. The diversity and versatility of your writing abilities and your insightfulness regarding business management and marketing never fail to knock my socks off, even after decades of working together. As always, Marcelle, I thank you for the time you take to truly listen and for the care and flair you put into telling the stories of my life at sea.

I submit a deep bow to Tricia Levi, my editor at Rizzoli, for her skill, her insights into what makes the difference between a good cookbook and an excellent one, and for all the work she has done to manage this project so beautifully. Of course, Tricia, I must also mention your infinite patience working around my travel schedule, and the other usual detours. *Millegraci.*

Again I am honored to continue producing such distinctive cookbooks with Rizzoli Publications. To my publisher Charles Miers, I salute your commitment to excellent content and production value. Cheers and well-done to the Rizzoli design team.

In a professional kitchen, nothing gets done well without solid leadership and nothing exciting is ever produced without brilliant leadership. Bearing this thought in mind, I tip my toque to the great leaders at Holland America Line who set the example of courage to venture forth boldly into uncharted waters: Stein Kruse, president and chief executive officer; Rick Meadows, executive senior vice president, marketing & sales; Dan Grausz, senior vice president, fleet operations; Judy Palmer, vice president, marketing communications; and Rose Abello, vice president, public relations.

A mere thank you doesn't seem sufficient to acknowledge Zane Tankel, Sigrid and Klaus Reisch, Fran Scott, Sirio Maccioni, and Mike Smith for their unwavering support. Your presence in my life means the world to me.

And, finally, to all of you who use this book, I raise my glass and toast you with the words of my young friend, Liam: "God bless the cook!"

RUDI SODAMIN
Master Chef, Culinary Consultant, Holland America Line

CONVERSION TABLES

WEIGHTS

AMERICAN	METRIC
⅛ ounce	3.5 grams
¼ ounce	7.5–8 grams
½ ounce	15 grams
¾ ounce	20 grams
1 ounce	30 grams
2 ounces	55 grams
3 ounces	85 grams
4 ounces (¼ pound)	110 grams
5 ounces	140 grams
6 ounces	170 grams
7 ounces	200 grams
8 ounces (½ pound)	225 grams
9 ounces	255 grams
10 ounces	285 grams
11 ounces	310 grams
12 ounces (¾ pound)	340 grams
13 ounces	370 grams
14 ounces	400 grams
15 ounces	425 grams
16 ounces (1 pound)	450 grams
1¼ pounds	560 grams
1½ pounds	675 grams
2 pounds	900 grams
3 pounds	1.35 kilos
4 pounds	1.8 kilos
5 pounds	2.3 kilos
6 pounds	2.7 kilos
7 pounds	3.2 kilos
8 pounds	3.4 kilos
9 pounds	4.0 kilos
10 pounds	4.5 kilos

TEMPERATURES

FAHRENHEIT	CELSIUS	GAS MARK
40	4.45	
50	10	
65	18.3	
105	40.5	
115	46	
120	49	
125	51.65	
130	54.4	
135	57.25	
150	70	
175	80	
200	100	0
225	110	¼
250	130	½
275	140	1
300	150	2
325	170	3
350	180	4
375	190	5
400	200	6
425	220	7
450	230	8
475	240	9
500	250	
525	270	
550	290	

LIQUID MEASURES

	FLUID OUNCES	MILLILITER
¼ cup	3	60
⅓ cup	4	80
½ cup	6¼	120
1 cup	12.5	240
1 pint (2 cups)	20	570
¾ pint	15	425
½ pint	10	290
⅓ pint	6.6	190
¼ pint	5	150
1 quart	50	960
1 gallon	200	3.84 liters
2 scant tablespoons	1	28
1 tablespoon	½	15
1 teaspoon	–	5
½ teaspoon	–	2.5
¼ teaspoon	–	1.25

LENGTHS

AMERICAN	METRIC
¼ inch	6 millimeters
½ inch	12 millimeters
1 inch	2½ centimeters
2 inches	5 centimeters
4 inches	10 centimeters
6 inches	15 centimeters
8 inches	20 centimeters
10 inches	25 centimeters
12 inches	30 centimeters
14 inches	35 centimeters
16 inches	40 centimeters
18 inches	45 centimeters

APPROXIMATE AMERICAN/METRIC CONVERSIONS

ITEM	USA	METRIC
Flour	1 cup / 4¼ ounces	115 grams
Granulated sugar	1 cup / 7 ounces	200 grams
Brown sugar (packed)	1 cup / 8 ounces	225 grams
Brown sugar (packed)	1 tablespoon / ½ ounce	15 grams
Butter	1 cup / 8 ounces	225 grams
Raisins (loose)	1 cup / 5¼ ounces	145 grams
Uncooked rice	1 cup / 7 ounces	200 grams
Cocoa powder	¼ cup / ¾ ounce	20 grams

INDEX